Redefining the Poverty Debate

T0097305

Redefining the Poverty Debate

Why a War on Markets is No Substitute for a War on Poverty

KRISTIAN NIEMIETZ

The Institute of Economic Affairs

First published in Great Britain in 2012 by
The Institute of Economic Affairs
2 Lord North Street
Westminster
London sw1p 3lb
in association with Profile Books Ltd

The mission of the Institute of Economic Affairs is to improve public understanding of the fundamental institutions of a free society, with particular reference to the role of markets in solving economic and social problems.

A CIP catalogue record for this book is available from the British Library.

ISBN 978 0 255 36652 6
eISBN 978 0 255 36682 3

Many IEA publications are translated into languages other than English or are reprinted. Permission to translate or to reprint should be sought from the Director General at the address above.

Typeset in Stone by MacGuru Ltd
info@macguru.org.uk

Printed and bound in Britain by Hobbs the Printers

CONTENTS

THE AUTHOR

Kristian Niemietz joined the IEA in 2008 as Poverty Research Fellow. He studied economics at the Humboldt Universität zu Berlin and the Universidad de Salamanca. In 2007, he graduated as Diplom-Volkswirt (MSc in economics), with a dissertation on the privatised pension system in Chile. During his studies, he interned at the Central Bank of Bolivia (2004), the National Statistics Office of Paraguay (2005) and at the IEA (2006). After graduating, he went on to work for the Berlin-based Institute for Free Enterprise (IUF). Kristian is currently a PhD student in public policy at King's College London, where he also teaches economics. His IEA monograph *A New Understanding of Poverty* was awarded the 2011 Templeton Freedom Award and the 2012 Arthur Seldon Award for Excellence.

AUTHOR'S ACKNOWLEDGEMENTS

I would like to thank Philip Booth, Peter King, John Meadowcroft, Séan Rickard and J. R. Shackleton for their highly appreciated feedback and suggestions.

FOREWORD

'Beveridge tells how to banish want. Cradle to grave plan. All pay – all benefit', read the front page of the *Daily Mirror* in 1942.

We were promised a revolution under which 'every citizen willing to serve according to his powers has at all times an income sufficient to meet his responsibilities'. But what started off as a safeguard to look after the poorest in our society has grown beyond recognition. Some thirty million people – almost half the total population – now receive income from at least one social security benefit. Expenditure on social protection represents by far the largest single area of government spending. In 2012/13, at £200 billion or almost 30 per cent of government spending, it is one of the highest levels in the world.

Does this mean we have conquered poverty? Far from it, argues Kristian Niemietz, the author of this monograph. He is highly critical of what he calls the 'anti-poverty lobby' and finds the current benefits system to be neither an adequate nor indeed an effective response. He rejects the view that the answer lies in increasing benefit levels. Helping the poor to free themselves from poverty should not be about absolving the individual from all responsibility and nurturing a culture of victimhood, entitlement and dependency. An undue focus on the level of actual support can perpetuate a cycle of helplessness. Beveridge identified idleness as one of the giant ills of modern society. The provision of social security has raised living standards, but it has also created a vacuum in which individuals most in need are no longer seeking to empower themselves.

The 1997 Labour government denounced the Tory legacy of one in five non-pensioner households having no one in work. It promised to make work pay, so that no household would be better off out of work than in work. It introduced tax credits and benefit tapers, as well as a minimum wage to provide a baseline, but, in terms of its strategy, it did not go much beyond looking at rates of benefits.

The experience of the US welfare-to-work programmes pointed to the dangers of a population of the 'working poor'. But it is wrong to paint low-paid work in a negative light. Being in work is as much about work as it is about social inclusion. Incentives to get the unemployed back into work should not be portrayed as exploitation or 'slave' labour. Some of the benefits that support low-earning workers such as working tax credit are shown to encourage greater reliance on the benefit system, rather than encourage work.

If increasing benefits doesn't deal with poverty, what does? The book makes a strong case for a radical, market-oriented approach. Make those things needed for basic living more afford-able by reducing their overall price. While this will help everyone, it will help the poor disproportionally more. But do we not need to protect the poor from the ravages of the market? Or can we harness the power of the market by challenging vested interests and monopolies?

At the root of post-war German success was the introduction of the social market economy championed by Ludwig Erhard. He wanted the German people to have as much economic freedom as possible, as this would lead to a fair and adequate distribution of the country's resources, while still providing for the poorest.

Despite expressed fears that this would make the poor poorer and the rich richer, he persisted. When Germany ended rationing (six years ahead of the UK) it set prices free, encouraged initiative and revived the economy. Erhard understood that government control could not work: government could never know enough to adequately allocate resources to deliver prosperity to everyone. Only the market could distribute wealth justly. As Erhard said: 'Need would be overcome through growth. Inequality would become irrelevant through growth. The market, because it provided people's needs, because it raised their standard of living, was social.'

Both Erhard and Beveridge understood and acknowledged the importance of work. For Beveridge the nation needed a national health service; tax-funded allowances for children and full employment to make social security work. For Erhard economic growth would make inequality irrelevant.

These concepts are as important today as they were then. The global financial crisis of 2008 has led some to associate capitalism with the causes of poverty. Hence tackling poverty has become synonymous with restraining capitalism.

This publication argues that anti-poverty measures that are potentially very cost-effective are overlooked simply because they run contrary to the received wisdom of governments and anti-poverty campaigners who focus only on income trans-fers. The author, Kristian Niemietz, provides a great service by dismantling the arguments of the poverty campaigners; chal-lenging the politicians; and making a strong case for a market-oriented anti-poverty strategy that will encourage work and raise real incomes. This is an important publication that deserves wide attention.

GISELA STUART
Member of Parliament for Edgbaston
November 2012

The views expressed in this research monograph are, as in all IEA publications, those of the author and not those of the Institute (which has no corporate view), its managing trustees, Academic Advisory Council members or senior staff.

SUMMARY

- In the past intellectual movements promoting free trade in particular and a free economy more generally were regarded as having a pro-poor agenda. The current poverty lobby, however, is focused entirely on government benefits as the solution to poverty and very rarely addresses government interventions that raise living costs. By way of example, when the debate about liberalising planning laws was at its height last year, all seven of the articles in the Child Poverty Action Group newsletter were about government benefits.
- Some progress was made in reducing poverty through increases in income transfers after 1997. Indeed, at the current time, the UK spends a greater proportion of national income on transfers than many Germanic and Scandinavian countries. Also, the extent of redistribution through state welfare systems is as great as that in Sweden. Furthermore, we have now reached the position where at least 68 per cent of all households with children in Britain are in receipt of one form of major transfer payment other than universal child benefit.
- Housing costs are a huge problem for the poor. Over the last 50 years, incomes before housing costs for the least well off have doubled. Incomes after housing costs, however, have

risen by only 60 per cent. The evidence suggests that high housing costs are largely policy driven.

- The poverty lobby's response to this problem is to propose extending housing benefit. It seems oblivious to the huge problems that this policy would cause. Increasing housing benefit would exacerbate the already very serious poverty traps as the benefit is withdrawn and increase housing demand (and therefore prices). It is a myth that our population density justifies the UK's restrictive approach to land-use planning. Reforming the planning system should be the focus of policy.

- Liberalisation of the planning system could reduce housing costs by around 40 per cent. However, planning reform needs to run with the grain of the market so that development decisions reflect the value of environmental amenities. This would involve localisation of planning responsibilities and tax-collecting authority.

- Food prices in the UK are considerably higher than in comparable EU countries. Again, restrictions on building are an important aspect of this as they reduce the productivity of the retail sector and reduce competition. Further reductions in food prices could be achieved by liberalisation of the Common Agricultural Policy. A conservative estimate suggests that policy changes could bring about a reduction in food costs of about 25 per cent.

- Policy reforms in other sectors could also bring about considerable benefits for the least well off. Specifically, childcare costs are very high in the UK compared with other European countries despite high levels of government subsidy; energy prices are raised by incoherent environmental policies; and many indirect taxes are especially targeted on products disproportionately consumed by the poor. It would be perfectly feasible to pursue the government's carbon-reduction policies in ways that increased energy bills by much less.

- Overall, a market-oriented anti-poverty policy could lead families to be up to £750 a month better off. There would also be scope for substantial decreases in taxation on the less well off because of substantial savings in benefits such as housing benefit.

- The UK is an outlier in terms of the failure of employment and family policy. Nearly 30 per cent of British children live in households with no adult in full-time work. Britain spends more on family benefits than virtually any other country in Europe. Furthermore, Britain is unique in Europe with its combination of high levels of single-parent families and high worklessness among single-parent families. The poverty lobby argues that there are high levels of poverty among those in work. While this is true for households where parents work part-time, poverty rates among families where one or two parents work full-time are low for single-parent families and negligible for two-parent families.

- These problems require a multi-pronged attack. Employment protection legislation – which tends to entrench long-term unemployment – should be liberalised; a new benefits system should remove penalties against family formation; effective marginal tax rates should be significantly reduced; and specialist assistance to those with weak labour market attachment should be managed and financed at local level. The government's much-trumpeted 'universal credit' will make little, if any, impact.

TABLES AND FIGURES

Redefining the Poverty Debate

1 ONE-CLUB GOLFERS – A CRITIQUE OF THE POVERTY INDUSTRY

Those underlings who in all the preceding ages of history had formed the herds of slaves and serfs, of paupers and beggars, became the buying public, for whose favor the businessmen canvass. They are the customers who are 'always right,' the patrons who have the power to make poor suppliers rich and rich suppliers poor.

LUDWIG VON MISES (1956)

Anti-poverty lobbies, then and now

In 1846, the British parliament decided to phase out the notorious Corn Laws, the scheme of import duties which protected cereal-producing landowners from foreign competition. The abolition of the Corn Laws, an important step towards a system of much freer international trade, was widely attributed to the relentless campaigning of the free-trade movement initiated by Richard Cobden and John Bright. The free-traders had not just provided an economic and moral case, but also succeeded in presenting their cause in terms of a particular narrative: 'a struggle between "the consumer and the aristocracy", rather than "labor versus capital", as the familiar rhetoric of the day coined it' (Leonard, 2010: 47). In essence, the Anti-Corn Law League's programme can be understood as a market-based anti-poverty strategy. Staple prices were of little importance to the better off, but made a difference to the living standards of those on the lowest incomes.

To an anti-Corn Law campaigner of that time, the accusation that free-market economics was an ideology that served a privileged elite – or 'the one per cent', in today's parlance – would have seemed bewildering. The assumption that an interventionist state was the natural ally of the poor would have seemed even more outlandish to them.

The 'Manchester School' considered itself a pro-poor movement, with an agenda favouring the underprivileged. Free trade was only the tip of the iceberg. The free-market programme meant opposition to any form of legal privilege for well-established market actors, who sought to protect their position from potential contenders. This applied to guild-style restrictions on entry into particular trades, monopoly rights, minimum prices or any other privilege obtained through political clout. It was a defence of the newcomer and the outsider against the politically well-connected insider. It would be wrong to describe their thinking as 'pro-business'. They had an intuitive understanding of what Milton Friedman would put into words many years later: 'With some notable exceptions, businessmen favor free enterprise in general but are opposed to it when it comes to themselves.'[1]

In today's climate of opinion, with anti-capitalist movements such as Occupy sailing on a wave of popular sympathy, it may seem odd in hindsight that a free-market movement would have thought of itself as an anti-poverty movement. But the track record of the ideas they stood for speaks for itself. In

---

1   Becker Friedman Institute for Research in Economics, University of Chicago (n.d.), 'Milton Friedman in his own words'.

the nineteenth century, the countries which had gone farthest in embracing free markets became the richest nations on earth (see Maddison, 2008). Crucially, the success of these market economies was not confined to raising average living standards; the rise spread to those in low-paid occupations (see Nardinelli, n. d.). Development came much more slowly in those parts of continental Europe which retained mercantilist and guild-style systems for longer. Free economies have historically shown a great potential for promoting overall economic progress while also ensuring that the resulting opportunities are widely accessible.

During the twentieth century, the same broad pattern has been repeated outside the Western world. The countries which were earliest and/or went farthest in embracing market-oriented reforms are the ones which enjoyed the most rapid pace of development, and subsequently the most pronounced fall in poverty. Summary measures of economic freedom are closely associated with real GDP per capita, real income of the poorest income decile, growth rates, and social indicators such as life expectancy and literacy rates (Gwartney et al., 2011: 20–24). This feature is shown in Table 1. The comparison between territories such as Hong Kong and Singapore on the one hand and Venezuela on the other is quite startling.

Economic development in itself has a strong pro-poor bias. As Milton Friedman (1980) explained: 'Industrial progress, mechanical improvement, all of the great wonders of the modern era have meant little to the wealthy. The rich in ancient Greece would have benefited hardly at all from modern plumbing – running servants replaced running water. Television and radio — the patricians of Rome could enjoy the leading musicians and actors in their home.' Nevertheless, advocates of free-market economics have

Table 1 **Changes in economic freedom versus changes in GDP and poverty**

	Economic freedom in 1975	Economic freedom in 2008	Real GDP per capita in 1975 (100 = Western Europe in 1975)	Real GDP per capita in 2008 (100 = Western Europe in 2008)	% of population lifted out of poverty over the past three decades (threshold: $2 per day PPP)
Chile	3.93	8.08	37%	61%	16% [since 1987]
China	4.23 (1980)	6.20	8% (1980)	31%	61%
Hong Kong	8.31	9.01	61%	146%	Not available
India	4.56	6.45	8%	14%	9%
Mauritius	5.21	7.61	35%	67%	Not available
Singapore	7.00	8.68	56%	130%	Not available
South Korea	5.37	7.39	28%	91%	Not available
Taiwan	6.10	7.54	31%	97%	Not available
Venezuela	6.11	4.28	91%	49%	−1%

Sources: Based on data from World Bank (2012a), Maddison (2008) and Gwartney et al. (2011)

always been concerned with issues beyond aggregate measures of wealth. Corn Law-style interventions are insignificant in terms of their impact on overall economic development; low staple prices are not a prerequisite for achieving a high GDP. But the free-trade advocates of the nineteenth century nevertheless felt so strongly about the issue that they adopted it as their flagship cause.

An emphasis on improving the situation of the least well off has a long history in free-market economic thought, and an impressive empirical record to go along with it. But, undeniably, free-market liberalism has long since lost the credibility as an anti-poverty force that it enjoyed in the days of the Anti-Corn Law League. Today, in public intellectual circles, free-market economics is at best associated with economic efficiency, fiscal prudence or monetary stability, but certainly not with poverty alleviation, neither in terms of global poverty nor in terms of domestic poverty in developed countries.

In the debate on global poverty, anti-globalisation groups enjoy a lead, as the success of best-selling authors such as Naomi Klein, Noreena Hertz, Noam Chomsky and Ha-Joon Chang demonstrates. For these groups, a market-based anti-poverty strategy is a contradiction in terms. Global capitalism is seen as the very cause of global poverty, so that 'tackling poverty' becomes virtually synonymous with restraining global capitalism.

The debate about domestic poverty in the UK does not show a comparable degree of militancy and ideological fervour. It is dominated by charity groups, not by strident NGOs. But it has one thing in common with the debate about global poverty: It is populated by people who share a deep-seated hostility to the market economy.

There is a vast network of anti-poverty advocacy groups in Britain today. End Child Poverty, an umbrella association, lists over 150 member organisations. Many anti-poverty groups are non-political; they are concerned with practical issues, or with general public awareness of the topic. But those which do openly express political views tend to be strongly anti-market. Publications by the Child Poverty Action Group (CPAG), the most overtly political organisation among the poverty activists, typically start with introductory remarks such as: 'The roots of the current economic crisis lie in deregulated economic policies that prioritised GDP growth over income and wealth distribution. Policies of "trickle-down economics" have left the UK a highly unequal country' (CPAG, 2009a: 2).

If poverty is interpreted as a by-product of the market economy, or at least of its 'excesses', then an anti-poverty strategy must necessarily be an anti-market strategy. The idea of a market-based anti-poverty strategy must then appear oxymoronic. In this worldview, the government is perceived as a benevolent agent which benefits the poor in principle, but which has an unfortunate tendency towards complacency. This is where the poverty campaign groups see their own role: to push the government out of its complacency and towards 'more action'. Up to a point, the policies advocated by these groups became the policies of the 1997 Labour government and its successors. Through the Child Poverty Act, these policies then became partially binding for the present coalition.

Wrong priorities in the poverty debate, and why it matters

In terms of policy solutions, the poverty activists are heavily fixated on public spending – cash benefits, in-kind benefits and social services – as a weapon against poverty. Policy options which do not fit into this framework are either not considered at all or, if they are, are squeezed into the same framework anyway. This has led to a debate with very limited breadth and scope, in which many potentially effective solutions can never be suggested in a debate about poverty simply because they do not match the way in which the debate is framed.

It is not just the campaign groups which fall into this trap. The same mindset pervades large swathes of poverty research. A case in point is the edited volume *Towards a More Equal Society?* (Hills et al., 2009), which can be considered a standard reader on British social policies since 1997. It provides a wealth of detail on the evolution of different transfer instruments and government programmes, covering areas from family benefits and pensions to health, discrimination and investment in deprived neighbour-hoods. The book is, on the one hand, impressively comprehen-sive – but it is, at the same time, astonishingly narrow, since it is wholly government-centred. It is a book on poverty as seen from Whitehall, and as dealt with from Whitehall. It describes the lives of those at the bottom of the income distribution as determined through the interplay of different government transfers and programmes. Other factors which have affected the living stand-ards of low earners are at best mentioned in passing.

This leaves a large blind spot. The period since 1997 has indeed seen a host of new policy measures to deal with poverty, alongside an expansion of previously existing ones, and there have indeed been partial successes. But it is also true that these successes have been offset – at least partially, if not completely – by misguided policies in other areas which depress the living standards of low-income households. This incoherence remains invisible when we reduce the poverty debate to a debate about social programmes and the transfer of incomes and the provision of services to the poor.

Nowhere is this incoherence more striking than in the area of housing. Housing costs have become one of the most pressing issues for low-income households. They are one of the major determinants of their living standards, which should make it an obvious focus of poverty activists. And yet, the way the activists have treated this issue has been, to say the least, unhelpful. The poverty campaigners are clearly aware of the housing affordability crisis; depictions of families living in conditions of overcrowding and decay feature heavily in their materials and rhetoric. But this is immediately turned into an agenda for more government activism: higher housing-related benefits; wider eligibility criteria; and an increase in public housing provision (e.g. Oxfam, 2010a; Oxfam, 2010b; CPAG, 2011, 2010a; CPAG, 2009a: 47–8). Given that spending on housing benefits is already at historical record highs, and that the social housing stock is already one of the largest in the developed world, these priorities are surprising. It would be a more obvious starting point to ask why housing costs have gone up so much in the first place. Their approach to housing is symptomatic of the anti-poverty lobby's approach to issues across the board: whatever the problem, the solution is seen as more public spending, more programmes and more initiatives. The questions of what has initially caused the problem, how much the government is already doing in this area and with what results are not asked. The lack of interest in wider underlying causes is typified in statements like: 'Investing in incomes gets at the root cause of poverty – low income' (CPAG, 2008: 9). But *real* incomes, of course, are determined not just by incomes, but also by prices, which may well be raised by government action.

Nevertheless, this present monograph is not a critique of

the poverty campaigners' work. Its emphasis is not on what the campaign groups say, but on what they do *not* say – on the elephant in the room in which the poverty debate takes place. There are potentially cost-effective anti-poverty measures which do not receive sufficient attention because they do not fit into the preferred pattern of large-scale, Whitehall-administered programmes. This frequently leads to missed opportunities.

The coalition's recent failure to tackle the housing crisis through a reform of the land-use planning system provides an example. In 2011, Minister Greg Clark launched the Draft National Planning Policy Framework (NPPF) (DCLG, 2011a), announcing an overhaul of the planning system to facilitate residential development. The proposals were very moderate, but at least they addressed the supply side of the housing market, which is where the problem of high house prices originates. Within days, an alliance of vested interest groups with an anti-development agenda was up in arms, launching a series of media attacks in order to bring the coalition's proposals down. With organisations such as the Campaign to Protect Rural England (CPRE), the National Trust, English Heritage and the Woodland Trust, as well as Greenpeace and Friends of the Earth, the interests of home-owners and conservationists are well represented in the political arena. In this situation, a genuine anti-poverty lobby should have seen as its natural role to act as a countervailing force, and articulate the interests of low-income families struggling with high housing costs. With the anti-development lobby trying to derail the planning reforms, a proper anti-poverty lobby would have pushed the government to go much further in permitting development, or at the very least to stand its ground. This would have meant a confrontation between the anti-development lobby

them almost entirely by moving no farther than to a neighbouring borough.

Of course, for a family rooted in its neighbourhood community and with children at a local school, this is still not an easy decision. It is also true that, in real terms, deeper cuts are likely to creep in over the next few years, because housing benefit rates will now be uprated by the Consumer Price Index instead of the Retail Prices Index. But the point remains that the key issue for housing affordability is planning reform, not housing benefit. The poverty campaigners wasted their political energy on the sideshow and ignored the main plot.

The same phenomenon reoccurs over a number of issues. Despite their good intentions, the poverty activists are so narrowly focused on raising benefits and expanding social services that they remain blind to potentially much more important issues. The UK's high cost of living is a part of their argument, but only insofar as it serves to underpin their calls for higher benefits. The main deficiency in the present poverty debate is not that there are too many 'wrong' ideas, but that there are too many blind spots.

The opposition to low-paid employment

There is a second set of reasons why the poverty debate needs a different focus. The strategy advocated by the poverty activists is, ultimately, a top-down strategy. In their worldview, alleviating poverty is something which is done *for* the poor, not with them, let alone *by* them. Poverty alleviation is seen as the responsibility of politicians and social workers; the participation of poor people themselves is not required.

This mindset finds its clearest expression in the activists' hostility to reform proposals aimed at ensuring that welfare recipients are active in some way in return for benefits. The idea that welfare should go beyond handing out money is always categorically rejected. According to CPAG (2008): '... [welfare] should be provided as a right to people who need that support, and should not be conditional on behaviours that may be difficult to achieve' (ibid.: 3). In a report on welfare reform, they say:

> CPAG has long argued that it is unjust to impose the greatest responsibilities upon the most disadvantaged groups who have the fewest rights, and that support should be extended to the most disadvantaged groups, irrespective of their work status, ability or willingness to engage in work-focused activities [...] The provision of much needed support for vulnerable groups should be provided irrespective of their 'behaviours' [...] CPAG does not think the provision of such support should be linked with 'greater responsibility'. (Ibid.: 7–8)

This is also the position of Oxfam (2010c):

> [P]eople who are new to, or re-entering, the labour market often have a range of difficulties and barriers that make holding on to a job particularly hard for them. A bad financial experience with work can lead to individual and 'folk' memories that – perfectly logically – militate against trying work in the future.

The benefits system, meanwhile, is presented as a viable alternative:

> Benefit levels are very low, and have been deliberately run down compared with wages over the past 30 years in order to make them more and more difficult to live on. However,

they afford people a stability of income that the modern labour market increasingly denies them. (Ibid.: 22)

The rejection of strategies to make benefit claimants more active is not limited to formal conditions and requirements. Even a non-binding encouragement to consider employment options for the future is already perceived as overexerting recipients. This can be seen in the responses to the Green Paper on welfare reform (DWP, 2008). It suggested that workless single parents with young children should be required to attend occasional interviews with a case manager, in order to discuss future employment options. In a report responding to the Green Paper, CPAG (2008) expressed fears that such proposals 'may have a negative impact on take up of support among some groups who may fear they are there to force them to access paid employment', and warned against 'using threatening language' (ibid.: 7–8).

What explains this opposition? One explanation is that the poverty activists are quick to suspect base motives behind such proposals. Seen in this light, terms which will look harmless to a casual reader (e.g. 'work-focused', 'responsibility', 'participation') become covert cues, whose 'true' purpose is to 'blame the victim' and stir up resentment. The campaigners' tendency to detect victim-blaming prevents them from differentiating between the pathways *into* poverty and the adequate pathways *out* of it. As Saunders and Tsumori (2002: 65) have pointed out: 'Even if all those who suffer disadvantage were to turn out to be victims of circumstances beyond their control, it would still not follow that the best strategy for helping them would be to absolve them of all responsibility for getting their lives back on track'. Or, in Murray's (1990: 85) words: '[E]ven if it is true that a poor young person is not responsible for the condition in which he finds himself, the worst thing one can do is try to persuade him of that'.

Another reason for the poverty campaigners' opposition to activation strategies is their animosity towards low-paid employment (or, in their own terminology, 'sub-prime jobs'). The world of low-paid work is always described in negative terms, associated with exploitation, insecurity, menial tasks, stress, time pressure and adverse impacts on family life (Oxfam, 2011; CPAG, 2010b, 2009a, 2009b). The advantages of work are not mentioned, let alone the possibility that a 'sub-prime job' could be a first rung on a ladder. Instead, Oxfam (2010c: 4) warns that 'taking on paid work can be a risk rather than an opportunity', and CPAG (2009b: 33) warns that 'precarious jobs that do not fit well with family life generate stress for parents and children'. Problematically, such descriptions of the risks and downsides of low-paid work are not balanced against the risks and downsides of long-term worklessness. The latter are well established (e.g. Kay, 2010), but play no role in the work of the poverty activists.

The working poor

One of the poverty campaigners' most oft-repeated arguments is that, owing to the existence of low-paid work, employment is, in the majority of cases, not a route out of poverty. Moving into work, they claim, merely means replacing one type of poverty with another, in most cases. Therefore, the policy focus on raising work levels is seen as misguided. Oxfam (2011: 4) claims:

> For the past 30 years, the political consensus has held that
> work is the best route out of poverty. And yet more than
> four million of the 13.5 million people who live in poverty in

the UK are working. [...] although work has been advocated as a route out of poverty, for many it does not provide economic independence and may actually damage their health and well-being.

CPAG (2009a: 1) also argues: 'Paid work has been lauded as the route out of poverty, but for the more than one in two poor children with a working parent, that promise has been false.' What they refer to here is the share of children in households below the relative poverty line (60 per cent of equivalised median income) who already have a parent in employment. If over half of all poor children already have a parent in employment, then what good can it do to raise work levels even further?

In addressing this claim, it is sensible, for the sake of the argument, to leave aside the question of whether relative poverty is really a meaningful concept. The figures cited by the poverty campaigners cannot be sensibly interpreted without keeping in mind that they treat work status as a binary variable. A household can only be 'out of work' or 'in work', without accounting for differences in weekly working hours or in the duration of employment among those working. This means that all those in minor employment, as well as those in short-term temporary employment, are counted as 'working poor'. Once a household has at least one adult in full-time, year-round employment, it is almost impossible to fall below the relative poverty line.[2] When figures on in-work poverty are presented without this context, they can provide the wrong impression that work in general mostly fails

---

2   It is possible to have a *market* income below this threshold, but this is not true for *disposable* income once working tax credit and, in the case of a household with children, child tax credit and child benefit are added.

to lift families out of poverty, and that there is not much point in even trying.

Poverty campaigners argue that, instead of pushing welfare recipients into the kind of jobs they could currently obtain, policymakers should 'create' better jobs, i.e. jobs that are more attractive, more secure and more highly paid. What they fail to see is that there is no conflict between these two aims. Surely all sides of the debate can agree on the desirability of labour market institutions which enable the creation of well-paid and fulfilling jobs. But this does not obviate the case for a welfare system that encourages and requires recipients to work. A robust anti-poverty strategy must not rely on ideal conditions. It must still be workable when employment opportunities, for whatever reason, fall short of the standards we would like to see.

There are occasional downturns even in the world's most smoothly functioning labour markets, and there are regional or industry-specific downturns all the time. A robust welfare system is one in which such developments do not lead to an escalation in the welfare rolls. One of the most well-established findings from labour market economics is that worklessness has a self-perpetuating tendency (e.g. Pissarides, 1992; Keane and Wolpin, 1997; Strulik et al., 2006; Ljungqvist and Sargent, 2008). After a longer time of detachment from the world of work, formal skills and work-related 'soft skills' decay, which makes it harder to re-enter the labour market once the downturn is over. Even if the government could 'create' secure and well-paid jobs and deliver them to everybody's doorstep, as the poverty campaigners seem to think it can, it would still not be advisable for the workless to sit back and wait until these jobs arrive. Even then, a low-paid job could be a stopgap or a stepping stone. If it provided no other benefits, it would still serve as a means to nurture work-related habits and to signal this to potential employers.

The poor are not helpless

The poverty activists advocate a policy strategy in which protection plays a large role, but empowerment plays virtually none. The contributions which poor people themselves can make to overcome their situation are played down, low-paid employment is denigrated, the role of work in overcoming poverty is trivialised, and attempts to encourage welfare recipients' participation are denounced as 'blaming the victim'. Meanwhile, dependency on government transfers is presented as entirely unproblematic if the transfer sum is adequately high. In what follows, it will be shown how this approach has reached its limits.

The state-centric poverty alleviation strategy: a fair-weather approach

Income transfers reduced poverty – for a while

In the late 1990s, domestic poverty became a top priority of the Labour government. This was not just political rhetoric. It led to the adoption of explicit poverty targets and of a comprehensive set of policy measures, which the present coalition has not fundamentally altered. It was a predominantly state-centric approach to poverty alleviation right from the start, and became even more so over time. The key ingredient was a strong expansion of cash benefits and publicly provided services (see Hills et al., 2009).

For a while, it seemed to work rather well. Up until about

2004, living standards of the least well off were rising, especially among families with children. As Table 2 shows, this was confirmed by a variety of indicators, not just the government's dubious relative poverty measure.

Table 2 **Living standards at the lower end of the distribution**

	1998	2004	2010
Annual median income in the bottom quintile, after housing costs, 2010 prices, equivalised	£6,760	£8,372	£7,852
% of population below 60% of 1998 real median income, after housing costs	24%	13%	15%
% of children in households below 60% of 1998 real median income, after housing costs	34%	18%	18%
% of children in material deprivation and in households with relatively low income	21%	17%	14%
% of pensioners below 60% of 1998 real median income, after housing costs	29%	18%	14%
% of households without central heating	11%	5%	5%*
% of households without a washing machine	8%	5%	4%*
Spending on housing (net of housing benefits), fuel and power, food and clothing as % of total expenditure, bottom income decile	49%	36%	40%

*Data from 2008
Sources: Data from ONS and DWP (2012b), ONS (2010), Brewer et al. (2008)

But, by 2004, the strategy had crossed its zenith. Since 2004, the living standards of the least well off have made little or no progress, so the turning point precedes the onset of the great recession. The only measure that still shows 'improvement' is relative poverty, which, between 2007 and 2010, fell from 22.5 per cent to

17.5 per cent among children, from 22.7 per cent to 17.5 per cent among pensioners, and from 18.1 per cent to 16.0 per cent among working-age parents (Cribb et al., 2012: 53). This was driven by the steep fall in median incomes in 2010, which dragged the poverty line down with it. It was not caused by an improvement in the position of the poor, but a fall in the position of everybody else.

Why did progress on raising low earners' living standards come to a halt in the mid-2000s? The poverty campaigners had difficulties explaining this since the strategy that had been pursued was, to a large extent, 'their own' strategy. The large-scale income-transfer programmes which they had long demanded had become a reality, putting them in the uncomfortable position of a political movement that witnesses the fulfilment of most of its aims. Within their framework, the only permissible explanation was that the government was still not doing nearly enough. The movement approved of the general direction, but it was described as no more than a good start (e.g. CPAG, 2009a).

When will the poverty lobby be satiated?

This raises the question of what level of poverty reduction, if any, would qualify as 'enough'. It is worth bearing in mind how far the attempts to alleviate poverty through government transfers have already been taken. For households in the bottom quintile of the income distribution, the government is the main breadwinner, with cash benefits representing by far the most important income source. This figure itself is not very different from that for previous decades. What is more remarkable is that, in the second quintile, cash transfers also contribute almost as much to total income as market earnings – these figures are shown in Figure 1. Even

Figure 1   **The share of different income sources in gross income by quintile**

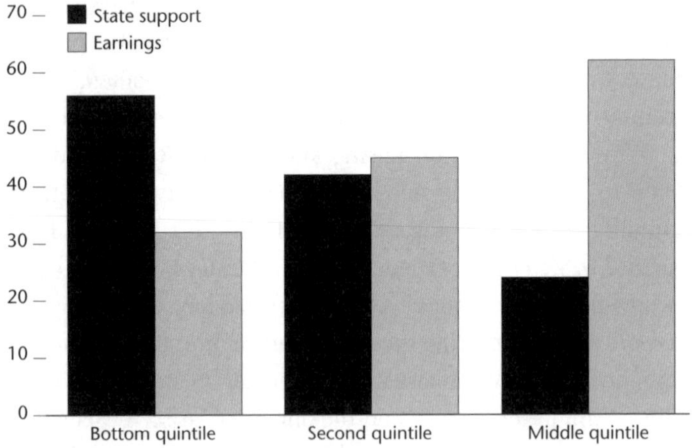

Sources: ONS and DWP (2012a: 36)

households in the middle quintile receive a quarter of their income directly from the state. It is only in the upper two quintiles that cash benefits can still be meaningfully described as 'income *supplements*'. The expansion of cash transfers has been strongest among families with children. At least 68 per cent of all children now live in a household receiving at least one major income transfer,[3] not counting the quasi-universal child benefit (ONS and DWP, 2012a: 110).

---

3   The major income transfers are child tax credit, working tax credit, housing benefit, income support, disability living allowance, jobseekers' allowance, and incapacity benefit/employment and support allowance. The qualification 'at least' refers to the fact that some of the remaining 32 per cent surely qualify for other, less well-known benefit types which are not listed in the Department for Work and Pensions Households Below Average Income (HBAI).

*We do not need to go to Scandinavia to experience
Scandinavian levels of income transfers*

The state has become a major income provider for well over half
the population, much more so, in fact, than these figures suggest.
First, these figures are based on household surveys, and it is well
established that the receipt of state transfers is heavily under-
reported. Secondly, the figures include only cash benefits, while
a large part of government provision takes place in kind, such
as implicit rent subsidies in social housing or free schooling and
healthcare.

Taking an international perspective, social expenditure
in the UK has reached Scandinavian proportions. In 2007,
net social expenditure[4] in the UK amounted to just under 23
per cent of GDP, more than in Norway and the Netherlands,
and not far below the Danish level (OECD, 2012).[5] Looking at
spending on family-related benefits in particular, the UK has
overtaken all the Nordic countries. These proportions seem here
to stay. Despite the ongoing controversies over 'austerity', public
spending in 2015/16 will fall back only to the levels last seen in
2007 (see Smith, 2011), and many areas of welfare spending have
been protected (see Niemietz, 2011). The conventional textbook

---

4   'Net', in this context, means net of direct taxes, because in some systems benefit
income is heavily taxed.

5   This is not a measure of welfare state 'generosity' per se, it is merely a large aggregate lumping very different spending items together. It reflects not only deliberate policy choices, but also exogenous variables like the old-age dependency
ratio, so total social spending would be a meaningless figure if societies with
vastly different age profiles were compared. However, on such demographic
summary indicators, the UK displays values which are very typical for a western
European country. If anything, it is noteworthy that the old-age dependency ratio
is slightly *lower* in the UK than in many neighbouring countries (see Eurostat,
2010: 25–27).

distinction between a high-spending 'Nordic model' and a low-spending 'Anglo-Saxon model' has become completely obsolete (if it ever was a useful concept) – this can clearly be seen from Table 3.

Table 3 **Social expenditure in the UK and the 'Germanic' countries, 2007**

	Net social spending as % of GDP (public and publicly mandated)	Family benefits as % of GDP
Austria	24.8	2.6
Denmark	23.9	3.3
Germany	27.2	2.7
Iceland	16.8	2.9
Netherlands	20.4	2.8
Norway	20.0	2.9
Sweden	26.0	3.4
Switzerland	n.a.	1.4
UK	22.7	3.6

Sources: OECD (2011a, 2012)

Separating fact from fiction

It is remarkable how little all this has affected the social policy debate. CPAG (2008: 18) continues to argue: 'There is political consensus around reducing child poverty and public support for meeting the 2010 and 2020 targets, the next step is for Government to mobilise the resources.' Polly Toynbee continues to explain: 'Nations can choose to be high tax, high social service, high social solidarity nations like the Nordics or they can choose to be the devil-take-the-hindmost US. Britain is heading down the American path.'[6] Or, on a different occasion: 'I want Britain to aim for the social and economic balance that thrives in Nordic nations', as opposed to 'all the neoliberal small statism wafting across the Atlantic, imbued with the Ayn Rand and Fox News meanness of spirit'.[7]

This strategy of denial is not limited to the conventional areas of cash-and-kind welfare spending. The idea that disadvantaged areas can be turned around through social investment programmes and social engineering projects has also been tried many times. Power (2009) summarises these policies in the following way:

> [The New Labour government] carefully targeted programmes at the most disadvantaged areas, setting up Health and Education Action Zones, welfare-to-work programmes, and Drug and Youth Action Teams. It continued the Single Regeneration Budget, [...] focusing government reinvestment through local partnerships on many of the poorest areas. It also announced initiatives for literacy and numeracy hours in primary schools, anti-crime initiatives, and a new regime of 'Tsars', such as 'Drug Tsars'. It was not always clear what the multiple zones and the hyperactivity of overlapping initiatives would do or who was really responsible for them, but they seemed to respond to a need. (Ibid.: 115)

And yet when the 2011 London riots broke out, commentators and social policy experts were quick to blame them on a lack of social initiatives.

---

6   Polly Toynbee, 'It's full-steam ahead for George Osborne's inequality drive', *Guardian*, 19 March 2012.
7   Polly Toynbee, 'Chris Grayling calls me a job snob for questioning those who pay so little', *Guardian*, 19 April 2012.

Has the income transfer approach failed?

Is it fair to say that the state-centric approach to poverty alleviation has failed? Some of its supporters argue that the strategy worked as long as it was pursued with full determination (Stewart et al., 2009; CPAG, 2009a). According to this argument, family benefits were raised at a rate that exceeded earnings growth up until the mid-2000s and, as a result, poverty fell. It was only when the government lost its stamina, and lowered the rate of increase in transfer spending, that poverty stagnated and finally rose again. According to this view, the strategy as such was a success, but the rate of acceleration was slowed down too soon. Stewart et al. (2009: 13) argue that the Iraq war and other events have distracted the government from its poverty agenda, competing with the latter for resources and attention. In their description, it appears as if the poverty strategy was initially successful, and was then slowed down by unfortunate coincidences and/or a lack of willpower.

Even accepting this interpretation for a moment, at least one major problem still remains: a policy which is so heavily reliant on politicians' continuous commitment is not a robust strategy at all. The political process is necessarily subject to mood swings. There is always a possibility of politicians suddenly discovering a new pet project, requiring new 'action teams', 'action zones', X-tsars and Y-targets, and government projects inevitably compete for resources. If this happens, the poverty activists have nothing to offer in reply. All their eggs are in one basket; their approach stands and falls with politicians' receptiveness to their concerns. It is not sustainable to devise a policy strategy which only works under the condition that politicians will always prioritise poverty alleviation above everything else. This is why this monograph concentrates on proposals which do not require the permanent attentiveness of politicians, but which can create a momentum of their own.

2 A NEW ANTI-POVERTY APPROACH

This monograph comes to conclusions that differ radically from the poverty campaigners' agenda, because it starts from a different premise. The poverty campaign groups never ask why there is such a high level of dependency on state transfers. They just take for granted that at least one third of the population[1] are chronically incapable of standing on their own feet. When taking this as a given and unalterable fact, permanently subsidising this part of the population must indeed appear to be the only feasible option. The rhetoric of reducing dependency must then appear as a mere excuse for an unwillingness to help.

In a highly developed and productive economy, however, most people should be quite able to attain a decent living standard through the means of market exchange most of the time – provided there are no unnecessary obstacles in place. If dependency levels are as high as they presently are, this indicates the presence of substantial obstacles. Anti-poverty policies should then, first and foremost, attempt to remove these. A safety net still has a role to play in this strategy, but it is a subsidiary one. Transfer payments would be the last step, not the starting point, let alone a substitute for everything else.

---

1   This is, roughly, the relative poverty rate that would result if it was based on incomes *before* social transfers, while treating state pensions as market income instead of transfers (see Eurostat, 2008: 150).

This monograph will identify two sets of obstacles. The first consists of misguided policies that inflate the cost of essential goods and services. Such inflators are present across a whole range of product markets, which cannot all be covered, but it is feasible to single out a few of the important ones. The second consists of welfare and labour market institutions that entrench worklessness and low work levels. To sum it up in one sentence, the alternative anti-poverty strategy proposed in this monograph is one of increasing work levels among the least well off, while simultaneously raising the purchasing power of their earned income through competitive product markets. This alternative would also require political will and tenacity. But it is not open-ended; it is a journey with an identifiable final destination. As such, it does not require never-ending political attention and dedication.

Reducing the cost of living – first do no harm

Various measures are proposed in the following chapters that involve radical, market-oriented reform that will benefit the less well off disproportionately.

In terms of the political dynamic of such an approach, it helps to use a parallel. The deregulation and denationalisation of the European aviation industry took several years, but once this was achieved, competition largely took care of the rest. Air travel then became steadily more affordable, the network of routes expanded, and market diversification increased. None of this required ongoing commitment from politicians; there were no 'affordability targets' and no 'Air Travel Action Groups'. On the contrary: progress was achieved against the political tide, which grew increasingly hostile to air travel as global warming became the new pet project.

Or, to use a comparison closer to the subject of this monograph: from 1995 onwards, the EU has been phasing out its textile quotas, which locked cheap clothes out of the European market. It did take longer than expected, and there were backlashes along the way. But in 2009, the quota regime finally came to an end, and once it was gone, the political appetite for bringing it back again faded. Even the European Apparel and Textile Federation, Euratex, has come to terms with these changes (Euratex, 2010: 1). For consumers, above all those on low incomes, this development has been a huge boon (see Francois et al., 2007). And unlike, say, the rounds of increases in tax credits, it continues to be a boon, even if political priorities have long moved on to other areas.

Removing welfare traps

The second set of obstacles is the poverty traps in the welfare system. Here, a similar logic applies. Once people have established themselves in the labour market, they have a degree of control over their income. There will always be declining industries, business closures, etc. But those who have no source of income other than government transfers are fully dependent on the whims of the political process.

Poverty campaigners and those sharing their mindset see this problem in principle, but cannot offer a solution. They are convinced that public opinion is hostile to welfare spending only because it has been 'manipulated' by the tabloid press and populist politicians. If only the press stopped talking about welfare abuse, the public would become more sympathetic to recipients, and supportive of increases in welfare spending. Caroline Lucas, MP (2012: 43) argues: 'when politicians and the media spend time attacking those in need – as during the Victorian age, and more recently from the 1980s onwards – the public's views can be shifted in the wrong direction'.

Horton and Gregory (2009: 210) blame the recent Labour government's attempts to limit welfare abuse:

> Sadly, however, these developments [increases in welfare spending] have been accompanied by a narrative about 'cracking down' and 'targeting benefit thieves' that has actually *reinforced* people's concerns about the integrity of the system. The result has been a vicious circle of further public anxiety and political pressure, met with further crackdowns, and so on. [...] Much better to say that fraud is low because people are basically honest and the integrity of the system is intact. (Emphasis in original).

In other words: pretend the issues do not exist, and the concerns will go away. But the key issue is that welfare entitlements are not contractual entitlements. They are merely promises, and can be changed by the political majority of the day. A robust anti-poverty strategy should concentrate on decreasing low earners' dependency on public sympathy, by decreasing their dependency on the state.

Taking on the critics

In short, this monograph makes the case for an anti-poverty agenda that gradually works towards its own redundancy.

To narrow its scope, the monograph will exclude areas where the aim of boosting low earners' living standards collides with competing valuable aims, and where very discretionary judgement calls would be required. It will single out market distortions that can also be criticised on other grounds. If a distortion depresses low earners' living standards while also creating problems in completely unrelated areas, and without generating substantial benefits, then removing the distortion comes as close as it gets to a win-win situation.

The monograph pools and bundles various well-established critiques of unnecessary market distortions. These critiques have mostly focused on how distortions affect overall economic efficiency and growth, a perspective which this monograph will complement by showing how economic reforms in these areas would help specifically those on the lowest incomes.

Of course, some will just dismiss the whole approach as a mere attempt to hide a market-oriented supply-side agenda under the cloak of poverty relief. For George Monbiot, for example, criticising green policies for their impact on low earners is per se dishonest and illegitimate when it comes from the 'wrong' political camp:

> Most of those making this argument do so disingenuously:
> they support the conservative or libertarian politics that
> keep the poor in their place. [...] promoting the interests of
> corporations and the ultra-rich under the guise of concern
> for the poor is an effective public relations strategy.[2]

The same goes for any critique of the land-use planning system: 'It's instructive to see how people with no record of concern for the poor become their champions as soon as there's something in it for the feral rich.'[3] This is a pity, because many

---

2   George Monbiot, 'Is protecting the environment incompatible with social jus-
    tice?', *Guardian*, 13 February 2012.
3   George Monbiot, 'This wrecking ball is Osborne's version of sustainable

of those proposing liberalisation have a strong record of real concern for the poor – and not just a concern that manifests itself in support for policies that involve redistributing other people's money. But even if the opponents of this strategy cannot respect the motives of its proponents, that is no reason to ignore the positive economic analysis of the benefits that a market-oriented anti-poverty agenda can bring for the poor. This market-based strategy is unveiled in the remaining chapters of this monograph.

development', *Guardian*, 5 September 2011. The 'feral rich' are housing developers.

3 HOUSING[1]

House prices on the rise

Over the past four decades, house prices have increased by a factor of about forty, while the overall price level has increased by a factor of about twelve (see Table 4). With differences in timing, rent levels have followed suit (Economist House Price Indicators, 2012).

Table 4 **Mix-adjusted house price index versus Retail Prices Index, 100 = 1971 levels**

	House price index	Retail Prices Index
1971	100	100
1981	472	369
1991	1,262	659
2001	2,133	855
2011	3,875	1,162

Sources: Based on data from DCLG (2011b) and ONS (2012)

In some senses, housing affordability is more relevant than house prices and rents. The standard measure of affordability is

---

[1]   This chapter is based on an earlier working paper by the same author: 'Abundance of land, shortage of housing', IEA Discussion Paper no. 38, Institute of Economic Affairs, London.

the 'median multiple' (MM), the ratio of median house prices to median annual gross income.[2]

Demographia (2012) provides data on median multiples for developed English-speaking countries, with both incomes and house prices collected at the regional rather than the national level. They show that the long-term average median multiple in English-speaking countries has generally clustered around a value of just below three. A family in the middle of the regional income distribution could thus afford a house in the middle of the regional price range by paying just under three times gross annual salary.

Today, there is not a single region in the UK which comes even close to this. Median multiples exceed a value of five in two-thirds of all UK housing markets. The phenomenon of runaway housing costs is by no means confined to London and the South-East. As can be seen in Table 5, it is a nationwide phenomenon.

This stands in stark contrast to the North American markets, where most regions still record median multiples below four, as was once the case in the UK. Even highly sought-after North American markets such as Miami, Boston, Seattle and Toronto record lower median multiples than most UK regions. Regions such as Washington, DC, and Chicago are more affordable than

---

2 The MM does not provide a complete picture. It contains no information about the cost of financing or the accessibility of housing credit, nor transaction costs. What it does show is housing affordability as far as it is determined by the housing market itself, not the credit or other adjacent markets. In this, it is superior to the alternatives. A simpler measure is the share of housing costs in total income, but this is misleading if people simply respond to a price increase by demanding less housing space. Also misleading is a measure of affordability based on the annual cost of mortgages. If inflation falls and so nominal interest rates fall, the cost of servicing a mortgage will fall but the real value of that mortgage will not fall as quickly as when inflation is high.

Table 5 **Median multiples in UK regions, 2011**

Median multiple	
4.0–4.9	Dundee, Falkirk, Leeds & West Yorkshire, Sheffield & South Yorkshire, Belfast, Derby & Derbyshire, Hull & Humber, Greater Manchester, Middlesbrough & Durham, Birmingham & West Midlands, Glasgow, Nottingham & Nottinghamshire
5.0–5.9	Cardiff, Blackpool & Lancashire, Leicester & Leicestershire, Northampton & Northamptonshire, Perth, Stoke on Trent & Staffordshire, Swansea, Liverpool & Merseyside, Newcastle & Tyneside, Warwickshire, Aberdeen, Newport, Edinburgh, Bristol & Bath
6.0–6.9	Exurbs of London, Warrington & Cheshire, Telford & Shropshire, Greater London
>7.0	Swindon & Wiltshire, Plymouth & Devon, Bournemouth & Dorset

Source: Data from Demographia (2012: 25–33)

any region in the UK. Only Australia shows a similar pattern of affordability as the UK. The British figures would look a lot worse still if they were adjusted for dwelling size or age.

Other data sets complement this profile. *The Economist*'s house price indicators (2011) are not given at the regional level, which makes them less insightful than Demographia's data. But *The Economist* data allow for a broader international comparison, comprising almost all Western countries. They show that, by international standards, the British house-price explosion, especially since the mid-1990s, represents an extreme outlier. Countries such as Spain, Ireland and the USA also experienced extreme increases for about a decade, but these were followed by sharp reversals after 2008. This did not happen in the UK, where real house prices have remained on the plateau they reached in the early 2000s.

All these figures refer to the cost of buying a house, but there is no principal difference in the rental sector. Table 6 below shows median rents in different categories, and the median income of tenants in the same category. The ratio of the two provides an idea of the proportion of tenants' income absorbed by rent payments.

Table 6 **Median rents versus median incomes in the rental sectors**

	Median annual rent	Median annual gross income	Ratio
Local authority	£3,588	£14,000	26%
Social housing association	£4,056	£15,500	26%
Private rental	£7,124	£23,200	31%

Sources: Data from ONS and DCLG (2012a)

Why are housing costs a problem?

Low incomes before and after housing costs

There is an ample literature examining the impact of high housing costs on general economic performance (e.g. OECD, 2011c). House prices do not just decrease overall living standards directly, but also demonstrably decrease labour mobility, and increase the likelihood of housing bubbles. But such considerations are tangential to this monograph. The main issue here is that high housing costs weigh most heavily upon the least well off. Middle-income households can respond, at least in the longer term, by cutting back on the quantity of housing space demanded, and this is exactly what they do. The average size of dwellings completed in the UK is much smaller than almost anywhere else in Europe (see Eurostat, 2010: 51). For average-income households in the

UK, high housing costs result in more constrained housing space rather than in higher housing expenses. But for low earners, the option of cutting back on housing space is not available to the same extent. There is a limit to how far downwards dwelling size can be adjusted.

The DCLG (2010) provides a formula to determine the minimum number of bedrooms which different household types 'need'. This so-called 'Bedroom Standard' is then used as a bench-mark with which the number of bedrooms households actually have is compared. If a household has fewer bedrooms than the formula, a dwelling is classified as 'overcrowded'. The Bedroom Standard is a crude measure of housing, and its thresholds are arbitrary. But since it is also a rather ascetic measure,[3] it can provide a rough-and-ready impression about constrained living conditions. According to this measure, 12 per cent of British children live in overcrowded conditions (ibid.: 26–9).

With scope for economising on housing space limited, escalating housing costs mean that low earners have had to reserve a steadily growing share of their income to meet housing expenses. This is illustrated in Figure 2, which shows the evolution of real incomes at the tenth percentile of the income distribution.[4] Incomes before and after housing costs (BHC and AHC) are

3   A very similar formula is used to establish entitlement to housing benefit, via the 'LHA Bedroom Calculator' (see LHA Direct, 2012).
4   The tenth percentile is a fairly good representation of the income situation of some of the least-well-off households in the country. Very low percentiles contain many people experiencing transitory low incomes, especially occupational groups whose incomes are volatile (e.g. the self-employed and freelancers). Yet Brewer et al. (2009) have plotted incomes against a variety of more direct measures of living standards, and found that those with the lowest living standards are clustered in an income range between 30 and 50 per cent of median incomes. The tenth percentile typically falls in this range.

shown separately. In the 1960s, incomes before and after housing costs rose at a similar pace. From then on, a gap opens between the two, showing low earners' housing costs increasingly eating into their budgets. During the 1960s and 1970s, households at the tenth percentile spent, on average, 20 per cent of their disposable income on housing. This share rose to 29 per cent in the 1990s and 2000s.

The comparison shows the centrality of housing costs as a determinant of low earners' living standards. The impression we obtain about how the least well off have fared over the past 50 years depends crucially on whether we look at incomes before or after subtracting housing costs. The former measure tells, by and large, a success story. Incomes before housing costs at the tenth percentile have nearly doubled in real terms and are now higher than median incomes in the early 1960s. Incomes after housing costs have also shown an upward trend, but, as Figure 2 shows, it is clearly a much less impressive one.

On expenditure-based measures of living standards, this impression is much stronger. A relatively straightforward measure is the family budget's share that has to be reserved for necessities (such as food and drink, clothing and footwear, housing and energy). On this measure, low-income households today appear better off than average households were even as recently as in the late 1980s, and much better off than average households in prior decades. Necessities occupy a smaller proportion of their budgets, freeing up more resources for items related to convenience, comfort and quality of life.

But there are large variations within the necessities category. Spending on food, drinks, clothing and footwear has plummeted to one fifth of the budget. Yet housing costs, broadly defined,

Figure 2   **Real incomes at the tenth percentile before housing costs (BHC) and after (AHC) in 2010 prices (£ per week)**

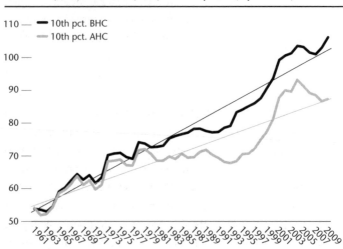

show a very different picture. Even after subtracting all housing benefit payments from rents (i.e. treating housing benefit as a rent rebate rather than as part of income), this category still accounts, on average, for just over a fifth of the budget, as shown in Table 7.

Housing benefit: a poor substitute for affordable housing

Housing affordability is a key topic for poverty and 'social justice' campaigners, but their work focuses almost exclusively on the symptoms of poverty. For them, apparently, the problem is not high housing costs per se, but a lack of adequate financial support from the government. A CPAG (2009a: 25–7, 47–8) report therefore advocates an extension of the housing benefit (HB) system

Table 7 **Spending on necessities: low earners today versus average earners in previous decades**

	All households 1967	All households 1977	All households 1987	Bottom decile only 2010
Food and clothing	36%	33%	25%	20%
Housing (net of housing benefit), fuel and power	18%	20%	22%	21%
Total necessities	54%	53%	47%	41%

through a removal of caps, a maximisation of take-up rates, and a less stringent targeting regime. In a Fabian Society report, Horton and Gregory (2009:146) argue:

> Part of the residualisation of housing provision has been the residualisation of financial support for housing provision, especially Housing Benefit, with its narrow coverage, inflexibility, and steep withdrawal rate. So part of our 'de-residualising' agenda has to be to extend this system of financial support.

Neither report addresses the question of why housing costs have escalated in the first place.

Effectively, these proposals represent an attempt to use the housing benefit system as a substitute for a functioning housing market. This approach is destined to fail. Nothing can replace a housing market that provides affordable accommodation to all levels of income. Pumping subsidies into a market with highly inelastic supply will merely raise costs further.

Indeed, the campaigners ignore how far the approach they advocate has already been taken. The housing benefit system is designed in such a way that coverage automatically increases when rent levels increase. Local housing benefit rates are set equal to rents at the thirtieth percentile of the local rent distribution. This means that, if rent levels rise at a faster rate than wage levels, more people become eligible. This is precisely what has happened, and as a result, the system is now bursting at the seams. Over the past two decades, total housing benefit spending has more than doubled in real terms. Despite all the controversial cost-containment measures, real-terms housing benefit spending in 2015 is forecast to remain above the level recorded at the onset of the recession (see DWP Statistics, 2011). The increase in total spending is the combined result of higher rates and a larger caseload. The share of households in Britain that receive housing benefit has risen to one in five – a total of 5 million households (ONS & DWP, 2012a). In the rental sector, the share is 44 per cent (see Table 8).[5] If this is 'narrow coverage', what coverage would count as a 'broad'?

Table 8 **Housing benefit dependency rate by tenure: share of households receiving housing benefit**

Private renters	25%
Social housing associations	60%
Local authority housing	65%
Total rental sector	44%

Source: Based on ONS & DCLG (2012)

But even ignoring the system's constraints, housing benefit payments or other forms of housing subsidies are not a viable alternative to affordable market rates. Since the government

5   Homeowners can also receive financial support with housing costs, but the coverage is much lower. The 44 per cent figure refers to England only, owing to a lack of nationwide data in the same format.

cannot pay everybody's housing costs indiscriminately, all housing benefit payments inevitably have to be targeted in some way. In the current system, this is done through means-testing. Housing benefit payments are withdrawn at a rate of 65 per cent as recipients' net income rises. The withdrawal rate implicitly acts like an additional tax on work, which undermines incentives to progress in the labour market. So, while the housing benefit system does indeed cushion the impact of rising rent levels on low-income households, it also penalises their work effort at the margin, and thereby produces a poverty trap. Furthermore, if pumping subsidies into the system simply raises rents (if supply is inelastic) it will raise housing costs for those just above the housing benefit level.

Poverty campaigners are fully aware of the poverty-trap effect caused by the housing benefit taper, but they seem to interpret this as a mere matter of design, which could be easily altered (see CPAG, 2009a: 47–8). If the taper rate discourages work, why not just lower it? But tinkering with the taper rate merely shifts the problem around. A lowering of the taper would widen the income range over which it applies. The work disincentive would be less extreme, but more people would be exposed to it.

This trade-off is, in principle, inevitable, but it becomes more and more unfavourable the higher the rent level is. This can be illustrated by a simple numerical example shown in Table 9. Suppose somebody qualifies for a housing benefit payment of up to £650, which is also exactly their monthly rent. For the sake of simplicity, it is assumed that they qualify for no other means-tested benefit.[6] They face a choice about their number of weekly working hours by working between zero and five days, but they

---

6   Accordingly, for purposes of illustration, 'applicable amounts' are not applied here. A small earnings disregard is however included.

cannot influence the hourly wage (£7.50). Column 2 shows the gross earnings resulting from different choices regarding the number of workdays, and column 3 the corresponding net income. If the recipient works for three days per week or more, the two no longer coincide, because the thresholds for income tax and national insurance have been crossed. Column 4 shows the housing benefit payment corresponding to each income level, and column 5 the resulting disposable income after subtracting the rent payment of £650. Column 6 shows the effective marginal tax and benefit withdrawal rate (EMTR) that applies when the recipient takes on one additional workday.

Table 9 **The impact of housing benefit withdrawal for a rate of £650**

Workdays per week	Monthly gross earnings	Monthly net earnings	Monthly housing benefit	Monthly disposable income AHC	EMTR
0	£0	£0	£650	£0	38%
1	£260	£260	£551	£161	65%
2	£520	£520	£382	£252	70%
3	£780	£741	£239	£330	76%
4	£1,040	£918	£124	£392	76%
5	£1,300	£1,095	£9	£454	76%

It shows that for a workless household, the incentive to enter minor employment is reasonably strong. Owing to the housing benefit earnings disregard and the personal allowance, the total effective marginal tax rate remains at a tolerable 38 per cent. But moving on from here, work is not financially lucrative, because the effective marginal tax rate then jumps to very high levels.

This is mainly because the housing benefit taper applies to the full income range that is relevant to this recipient. Housing benefit is fully tapered away at a gross income of just over £1,300, i.e. just above the maximum income this recipient can attain.

Now suppose the housing benefit taper rate was lowered by, for example, 15 percentage points, from 65 per cent to 50 per cent. For the recipient in the above example, this would lower the effective marginal tax rate from 76 per cent to 66 per cent. But housing benefit would now be extended to households with gross incomes of up to £1,750. For those earning above £1,300 and below £1,750, the effective marginal tax rate would jump from 32 per cent to 66 per cent. To put it simply, effective marginal tax rates would have fallen a bit for one group, but increased a lot for another. At the policy level, this is a very poor bang for the buck: 66 per cent would still be a very high effective marginal tax rate, and it would now apply to many more people, because the income range in question is a densely populated one.[7] This example demonstrates that with rents (and thus housing benefit rates) at this level, detrimental anti-work incentives are inevitable. Fiddling around with the taper rate can only distribute the burden differently.

The monthly housing benefit rate from this example is far from unusual. Table 10 shows housing benefit rates for a two-bedroom flat in twenty large British cities, which, taken together, comprise about one tenth of the housing benefit caseload. A couple or single parent with one child will typically qualify for these rates; larger households can qualify for much higher ones, so that the described anti-work effect is much stronger.

Expensive housing makes detrimental anti-work incentives inevitable. But the same argument also holds in reverse. There are very few places in the UK where the full housing benefit rate for

---

7   About half of the population live in a household with an equivalised disposable income between 60 and 120 per cent of the median.

Table 10 **Housing benefit rates in twenty cities**

	Monthly housing benefit rate for a two-bedroom flat (= rents at the 30th percentile)	Monthly gross income at which housing benefit is fully tapered away
Bournemouth	£650	£1,320
Brighton and Hove	£800	£1,660
Bristol	£625	£1,260
Cambridge	£585	£1,170
Canterbury	£625	£1,260
Colchester	£550	£1,090
Eastbourne	£650	£1,320
Exeter	£600	£1,210
Leeds	£532	£1,050
Luton	£575	£1,150
Milton Keynes	£625	£1,260
Oxford	£800	£1,660
Portsmouth	£600	£1,210
Reading	£795	£1,650
Slough	£800	£1,660
Southampton	£650	£1,320
Southend-on-Sea	£635	£1,290
Southern Greater Manchester*	£550	£1,090
Swindon	£530	£1,050
Woking	£895	£1,870

* The areas over which housing benefit rates are calculated do not always coincide with local authority boundaries. Greater Manchester is split into two parts with slightly different housing benefit rates.
Source: Author's calculations based on data from LHA Direct (2012)

a two-bedroom flat falls below £400 per month. But it is worth-while showing how work incentives differ with rent levels at this order of magnitude. Table 11 shows exactly the same example as above, except that the recipients' monthly rent and the full housing benefit rate are now assumed to be £400.

Table 11 **The impact of housing benefit withdrawal for a rate of £400**

Workdays per week	Gross earnings	Net earnings	Housing benefit	Disposable income AHC	EMTR
0	£0	£0	£400	£0	38%
1	£260	£260	£301	£161	65%
2	£520	£520	£132	£252	66%
3	£780	£741	£0	£341	32%
4	£1,040	£918	£0	£518	32%
5	£1,300	£1,095	£0	£695	32%

It is the same taper rate of 65 per cent of net income, but it is now much less damaging, because the income range over which it applies is much shorter.

The issue of runaway housing costs must be dealt with directly and at the source, not through the housing benefit system, which cannot act as a replacement for a functioning housing market. On the contrary, the fact that so many households are in receipt of housing benefit, and thus faced with strong work disincentives, must be interpreted as one of the adverse knock-on effects of the housing cost escalation. If rents were to drop to reasonable levels, some combination of the following beneficial effects would occur: a lot of housing benefit recipients would be taken out of the taper, as they would not need housing benefit any more; the housing benefit taper could be reduced; housing costs for the poor would fall; housing costs for those just above the housing benefit levels would fall; the taxes necessary to finance housing benefit would be reduced. This would also substantially improve work incentives – and probably the incentive to save given the impact on pensioners.

Social housing:[8] another poor substitute for affordable housing

In so far as poverty campaigners address the supply side of the housing market at all, they refer to state-provided housing, and housing provided by registered social landlords. CPAG (2012) speaks of a 'failure to maintain sufficient supplies of social housing', a view which is widespread beyond their camp. According to the British Social Attitudes Survey, one in five respondents believe that the best way to make housing more affordable is to increase the stock of social housing (DCLG, 2011a). The problem, in this interpretation, is not an overall shortage of housing, but a shortage in *one specific sector* of the housing market.

But what is true for the housing benefit system is also true for the social housing system: it cannot act as a substitute for a functioning housing market. In the first place, increasing social housing while restricting new housing development overall merely shuffles housing around. Private rented housing for the less well off may become scarcer (see Sinai and Waldfogel, 2005). But even ignoring this possibility, increasing social housing is no panacea – or even a partial solution.

First, like housing benefit, social housing is part of the poverty trap. It has locked many residents in areas with poor job prospects, poor educational opportunities and, above all, characterised by adverse peer-group effects. The result is low levels of labour market attachment among tenants and low levels of educational attainment among their children, even after controlling for

---

8   The question 'what is a social house and what is a non-social house' might be asked. By 'social housing' we normally mean housing that is subsidised or regulated by local authorities or bodies to whom the power is contracted out. The term 'social housing' has become common in the UK.

other factors. A social housing tenant is only half as likely to be in employment as somebody with similar socio-economic characteristics living in a different tenure, and their children are twice as likely to drop out of school without a qualification. A similar gap emerges for long-term and intergenerational indicators (Hills, 2007: 111; Leunig, 2009: 20; Greenhalgh and Moss, 2009). So proposals to expand this sector even further, and use it as a surrogate for the regular housing market, should be received with caution.[9]

On a more basic level, what supporters of this position fail to acknowledge is that the British social housing sector is already one of the largest in the developed world (see Table 12). Social housing accounts for one fifth of the total dwelling stock, slightly above Scandinavian levels, and well ahead of most of continental Europe.

The belief that the British social housing stock is exceptionally small is derived from a comparison with the 1970s and early 1980s, when the sector accounted for as much as one third of the total housing stock. Since then, the 'Right to Buy' privatisation programme has gradually reduced its share to the present level. But it is superficial to see this as a reduction in housing subsidies.[10] It is more adequate to describe it as a conversion of one

---

9 Supporters of social housing acknowledge these effects, but argue that they are due to the system's current design, rather than anything inherent in this tenure (Horton and Gregory, 2009: 36–9). In their interpretation, it is the need-based allocation system which concentrates social housing on the weakest groups, creating the negative peer-group effects.

10 This view is espoused by Polly Toynbee, who claims that '[s]ince 1980, when the Thatcher policy began, a net total of 750,000 council homes have been lost – the number sold without replacement' (Polly Toynbee, 'It's on the house', *Guardian*, 11 October 2002). What Toynbee overlooks is that these 'lost' homes continued to house low-income families on a subsidised basis.

Table 12 **Social housing stock as a percentage of the total housing stock, 2008 or latest available year**

	Social housing as % of total housing
Netherlands	32%
Austria	23%
UK	20%
Denmark	19%
Sweden	17%
France	17%
Finland	16%
Ireland	8%
Belgium	7%
Slovenia	6%
Germany	5%
Italy	4%

Source: Data from Eurostat (2010: 67)

type of subsidy into another. Council house tenants receive an implicit subsidy, which is the difference between the rent they pay, and the market rate. Council house buyers under the 'Right to Buy' programme also receive an implicit subsidy, which is the difference between the price they pay and the market price. On the basis of this implicit subsidy, buyers have become home-owners, many of whom can now live rent-free. The programme has reduced the supply of social housing, but it has also reduced demand for it.

To summarise, the problems in the housing market have nothing to do with a specific lack of social housing. The 'Right to Buy' has merely replaced subsidised tenancies with subsidised home ownership, and the remaining social housing stock is still one of the largest among developed countries. Social housing is clearly under immense strain. In England alone, 1.84 million households are currently on waiting lists (ONS & DCLG, 2011). But it is under strain because of a *general* shortage of inexpensive housing across *all* tenures. The sector is under strain because so many low-income households have been priced out of the conventional rental market, not to mention priced out of the option of ownership. The high level of reliance on social housing is another knock-on effect of the overall housing cost escalation, and it has itself become part of the problem, as social housing has become a poverty trap.

Knock-on effects: higher prices across the board

The effects of a constrained property market ricochet through many other sectors of the economy. Commercial rents, especially in space-dependent sectors such as retail, are reflected in consumer prices. Productivity in these sectors drops, as outlets are squeezed into locations which are less suitable from a business

Table 13 **Cost of a food basket* in western Europe, 100 = Irish level**

Ireland	100
France	107
Netherlands	109
Germany	110
Spain	111
Italy	111
Sweden	113
Denmark	116
UK	129

Source: Based on data from uSwitch (2011)
*The basket contains bread and cereals, meat, fish, milk, cheese, eggs, oil, fruit, vegetables, sugar, jam, honey, chocolate and confectionery.

perspective. The relationship will be explored further below. For now, however, it suffices to point out that the cost of a standard food basket in the UK is far higher than in most neighbouring countries (see Table 13).

The implications for the living standard of low earners need no spelling out. High housing costs affect low-income households in a multitude of ways.

What is going wrong?

The importance of planning laws: a literature review

Demographia distinguishes between two types of land-use planning regimes according to their default option. In restrictive systems, development is prohibited unless specifically allowed. In permissive systems, development is generally allowed (subject, of course, to environmental regulation, etc.) unless specifically prohibited. In their sample, none of the markets governed by a permissive regime has a median multiple above 4.0, while most of the markets governed by a restrictive regime have. For them, the case is clear: regulation drives up house prices.

But even though the figures seem to confirm this case neatly, the reasoning is inadequate. Planning regimes differ on many more dimensions than just their default option, and housing costs have many other potential determinants. On the demand side, trends in household size, immigration, labour market conditions, the development of wages and the availability of housing finance credit are among the obvious candidates. On the supply side, topography and natural obstacles, the extent to which an area is already built up, the state of the pre-existing housing stock and the market power of developers and/or construction companies come to mind. Over the last few decades, a substantial body of econometric literature has evolved to disentangle the impact of these different potential determinants, to estimate their relative importance and establish how they interact. These studies typically take some measure of housing costs, for example real-term house prices, real-term rents or the median multiplier, and express it as a function of a set of explanatory factors. Since about the 1980s, most of the literature has included some composite index of the restrictiveness of regulatory constraints.

Naturally, there is some disagreement in the literature. This is unsurprising given that the severity of regulatory obstacles is notoriously difficult to measure (see Quigley and Rosenthal, 2005, for a discussion). But given these difficulties, there is a remarkably high degree of agreement that regulatory constraints are an important determinant of housing costs. The disagreement is mostly about the relative importance of planning constraints when compared with other factors; the precise channel through which regulation exercises its impact; and which precise types of regulation are most costly. The anti-development lobby, predictably, denies this and insists that there is 'no evidence' about the impact of planning on house prices (CPRE, 2006: 17). But this position can be maintained only when ignoring the literature on the subject in its entirety.

Already in 1990, Brueckner (1990) was summarising the state of the evidence in the following terms: 'There is now a large empirical literature documenting the effects of growth controls on housing and land markets. The evidence to date conclusively establishes that growth controls raise housing prices in communities where they are imposed' (ibid.: 327). Since then, these findings have been strengthened and reinforced. Pollakowski and Wachter (1990) have modelled the determinants of house prices in Montgomery County, Washington, DC, and found: 'The results of our study confirm results found elsewhere: land-use regulations raise housing and developed land prices within a locality' (ibid.: 323). Malpezzi's (1996) cross-sectional study, which covers over fifty US metropolitan housing markets, finds: 'Our results suggest that regulation raises housing rents and values' (ibid.: 236).

Dawkins and Nelson (2002) provide a more cautious literature review, pointing out that other factors also matter. On balance, though, these authors also conclude: 'The most important policy implication to be gleaned from this review is that local planners play a significant role in determining the severity of housing price inflation attributable to urban containment policies' (ibid.: 11).

Saks (2005) looks at several metropolitan markets in the USA, and states: 'Raising the degree of housing supply regulation by one standard deviation results in 17 per cent less residential construction and twice as large growth in housing prices' (ibid.: 21).

Glaeser and Gyourko (2003) model house prices in 45 US metropolitan markets, with a particular emphasis on the importance of planning restrictiveness relative to scarcity of suitable land. They find:

> The bulk of the evidence marshalled in this paper suggests that zoning, and other land-use controls, are more responsible for high prices where we see them. [...] Measures of zoning strictness are highly correlated with high prices. Although all of our evidence is suggestive, not definitive, it seems to suggest that this form of government regulation is responsible for high housing costs where they exist. (Ibid.: 35)

Anthony (2003) estimates the effect of the 'Growth Management Act', a set of planning restrictions and regulations covering the whole state of Florida. He concludes:

> Using data from the entire state over a 16-year period, with two measures of affordability and after controlling for alternate hypotheses, this research finds that Florida's GMA has had a statistically significant and negative effect on housing affordability in the state.

Glaeser et al. (2005a), using a broad data pool of US metropolitan areas, find:

> new construction has plummeted and housing prices have soared in a small, but increasing number of places. These changes do not appear to be the result of a declining availability of land, but rather are the result of a changing regulatory regime that has made large-scale development increasingly difficult in expensive regions of the country. (Ibid.: 20)

The OECD, in an international comparison of housing policies and their evidence base, also points out: 'there is an emerging consensus that local land-use regulation has become a binding constraint on the supply of new housing units in some countries'. They caution, however, that 'there is much less of a consensus on the magnitude of the impact' (Andrews et al., 2011: 30).

The above-mentioned studies examine larger areas containing many different housing markets. Case studies focusing on one single housing market can also be insightful when well selected. Glaeser et al. (2005b) concentrate on housing costs in Manhattan, which represents an especially insightful case study because it makes alternative explanations (scarcity of developable land and high demand) more plausible than in almost any other housing market in the world. Even for this rather extreme case, however, the authors find that regulatory constraints are a more important determinant of prices than scarcity of space, high demand or market power in the building industry: 'one-half or more of the value of a condominium can be thought of as arising from some type of regulatory constraint preventing the construction of new housing' (ibid.: 367).

The case study by Chi-man Hui and Sze-mun Ho (2002) can be seen in the same light, because it concentrates on the extreme example of a housing market faced with an exceptionally high population density, natural obstacles to outward growth, and high demand: Hong Kong. Again, even in this unusual case, the authors find: 'The analysis demonstrates that most of the planning variables affect housing prices statistically' (ibid.: 357).

Cox (2011) argues that many previous studies, even though they confirmed that planning constraints were an important factor, have still tended to overestimate the importance of natural constraints. His observation is that, when growing cities have approached politically imposed growth boundaries, house prices have tended to escalate suddenly and rapidly, not gradually. Thus, studies which incorporate natural obstacles located a considerable distance from the urban fringe may have 'over-controlled' for those factors. They mistook non-binding natural constraints for binding ones, and ascribed to them a share of the house price inflation that should really have been ascribed to the planning system.

Since the above-mentioned models control for a wide range of factors, they are in principle transferable to other contexts. But to gain an appreciation of the magnitudes involved, the study by Hilber and Vermeulen (2010) is of particular interest because it refers to UK markets only. This study also places a strong emphasis on separating the impact of regulatory constraints from topographic ones, while also controlling for the extent to which an area is built up already. They find:

> a substantial impact of regulatory supply constraints: house prices in an average local planning authority in England in 2008 would be 21.5 to 38.1 per cent lower if the planning system were completely relaxed [...] Physical supply constraints matter as well, although the impact is more modest. (Ibid.: 56)

As the authors acknowledge, it is highly likely that their study substantially underestimates the impact of planning restrictions. Firstly, they make the simplifying assumption that no binding planning controls existed in the base year of their study, 1974. In this study, therefore, phrases such as 'if the planning system were completely relaxed' have to be interpreted as 'if the planning system were no more binding than it was in 1974'. This nuance matters. The systematic increase in the price of land began in the late 1950s and early 1960s (Hartwich and Evans, 2005: 17). Secondly, the model assumes that, once a plot is built upon, it is no longer available for development of any kind. This means that the role of height restrictions in preventing vertical extensions cannot be accounted for, so that one channel through which the planning system affects housing costs is omitted. It is also noticeable that the study is quite generous in its definition of 'natural obstacles'. The possibility that, in a more liberal planning regime, some of these constants could be turned into variables – e.g. steep slopes that could be levelled – is also not taken into account.

Cheshire et al. (2011) have modelled the impact of planning

restrictions in England on productivity in the retail sector, and find several negative effects. Planning restrictions lead to a more fragmented retail structure with smaller average store size, which reduces the exploitation of economies of scale. It also means that the choice of location often follows political rather than commercial considerations: retail outlets are opened where the retailer can obtain planning permission, rather than where it would make sense from a business perspective. The authors estimate that planning restrictions have decreased total factor productivity in the English supermarket sector by about one quarter since the late 1980s. This is a conservative estimate which does not take account of the extent to which retail productivity was already affected by the planning system at that time. These findings would go a long way towards explaining the aforementioned high price level for items such as food.

In summary, there is overwhelming empirical evidence that planning restrictions have a substantial impact on housing costs – but also on the costs of other goods such as food. Indeed, planning restrictions may well be the single most important determinant of housing costs. Even in very densely populated and built-up places, regulatory restrictions have been found to have a decisive impact on housing costs. High housing costs are not simply signals of scarcity. They are the result of policy choices, which are alterable and reversible.

The housing debate in the UK: myths, half-truths and red herrings

The above section has summarised the empirical literature which tries to isolate the impact of regulatory restrictions on

Table 14 **Regional population density in the UK, the Netherlands, Belgium, Switzerland and Germany**

	Inhabitants per km²
South Holland (NL)	1,254
North Holland (NL)	1,008
Utrecht (NL)	887
Zug (CH)	535
Basel-Landschaft (CH)	527
North Rhine-Westphalia (DE)	524
Limburg (NL)	522
Noord-Brabant (NL)	499
Flanders (BE)	462
Aargau (CH)	430
South-East (UK)	425
West Midlands (UK)	410
Saarland (DE)	398
Overijssel (NL)	341
Yorkshire and the Humber (UK)	327
Solothurn (CH)	320
Baden-Württemberg (DE)	301

Sources: ONS (2006), Centraal Bureau voor de Statistiek (2011), Statistische Ämter des Bundes und der Länder (2011), Research Centre of the Flemish Government (2011), Bundesamt für Statistik (2009)

development, controlled for other factors. What is lacking in the policy debate about housing is a sense of the exceptionality of the UK as compared with other countries.[11] The house price escalation is too often blamed on factors that are present in dozens of other countries as well (e.g. DCLG, 2011a), including in countries where real-terms house prices are still at the same level as 40 years ago.

An example of this is the focus on population density,

11 With Australia also being an exception.

Table 15 **Surface area of England by land use**

	England (% of area)	South-East (% of area)	West Midlands (% of area)
Green space and water	90.1	84.7	88.8
Domestic gardens	4.3	6.3	4.9
Transport routes	2.5	2.7	2.7
Buildings	1.8	2.0	2.1
Other/unclassified	1.4	1.6	1.5
Total	100	100	100

Source: Based on data from the DCLG (2007)

sometimes linked to immigration.[12] Table 14 shows population density figures for the most populous regions of the UK, the Netherlands, Belgium, Germany and Switzerland, excluding those that consist of a single city or conurbation.[13]

Greater London is obviously in a different league, but the population density figures for other UK regions are not unusual at all in comparison with other parts of Europe.

A closely related claim is about the alleged threat to the countryside. CPRE (2006: 5), for example, claims that '[a]cross large parts of England, especially in the South East, the spread of urbanisation means there is little "deep" or "real" countryside left'. Data from the Land Use Database, however, show that only one tenth of the English surface area is developed at all. The rest mostly consists of woodland, grassland and farmland. Even within the developed tenth, the single biggest item is gardens (see Table 15). Land which is literally 'concreted over', i.e. covered

---

12   'England is most crowded country in Europe', *Daily Telegraph*, 16 September 2008.
13   This results in the exclusion of Berlin, Hamburg, Bremen, Geneva, Zurich, Basel-Stadt and London.

with buildings, industrial structures, streets, roads, parking sites, rail tracks, etc., accounts for a mere one twentieth of the whole English surface area. These figures are not fundamentally different even when looking at the UK's most densely populated regions, the South-East and the West Midlands, in isolation.[14]

The UK National Ecosystem Assessment provides an alternative classification which covers the nation as a whole. It provides greater detail on the undeveloped and less detail on the developed parts, but the implications are the same. Overdevelopment is the very least of all risks (see Table 16).

Table 16 **Surface area of the UK, alternative classification**

	UK (% of area)
Farmland	41.3
Heaths, mountains, moorland	18.6
Grassland	16.4
Woodland	11.6
Urban	6.8
Coastal margins, waters & wetlands	2.7
Unclassified	2.6
Total	100

Source: Gathered from UK National Ecosystem Assessment (2011: 60–66)

Neither is there anything exceptional about the UK's demographic trends, such as the smaller average household size. Average household size in all north-western European countries except Ireland falls within a range of 2.0 to 2.5, and so does the UK's figure of 2.1 (OECD, 2011a: 19).

14   The area of Greater London, of course, is a very different matter.

Calls for tougher regulation of the rental market, advocated in papers as far apart as *The Economist*[15] and the *Guardian*,[16] are merely attempts to ban particular symptoms of the overall housing shortage. If implemented, these calls would lead to policies that are not just ineffective but actively harmful. The OECD shows that indicators of rental market regulation are negatively associated with indicators of the quality and availability of rental housing (ibid.: 18–19). Far from 'protecting tenants', rental regulation decreases the willingness of potential landlords to offer their property to the market for rent.

A further set of arguments tries to portray the housing shortage as a distributional issue: some people are constrained in the amount of housing space they can have because others have too much. George Monbiot, for example, proposes the use of 'housing footprints':

> While most houses are privately owned, the total housing stock is a common resource. [...] Your housing footprint is the number of bedrooms divided by the number of people in the household. Like ecological footprints, it reminds us that the resource is finite, and that, if some people take more than they need, others are left with less than they need.

Monbiot advocates a policy of government rationing of housing, on the basis that '[N]early 8m homes – 37% of the total housing stock – are officially under-occupied'.[17]

The figures come from the English Housing Survey (ONS

---

15 'Down and out in London. Newham cracks down on Dickensian housing conditions', *The Economist*, 31 December 2011.

16 Angela Phillips, 'Why I like the subsidised neighbours', *Guardian*, 1 November 2010.

17 George Monbiot, 'Let's take the housing fight to wealthy owners with empty spare rooms', *Guardian*, 4 January 2011.

& DCLG, 2010), which uses a formula to determine how many bedrooms different household types need. It is similar to the formula establishing how many bedrooms housing benefit recipients are entitled to, so it is not overgenerous. The actual distribution of the housing stock is then compared with this benchmark of need, and the results are unspectacular: 3 per cent of all households fall short of this standard, 25.4 per cent have exactly as many rooms as they 'need', 35.4 per cent have one more room than they 'need', and 36.1 per cent have at least two more than they 'need'. These figures refer to the national level, with a decomposition revealing a much narrower distribution of the housing stock at the regional level.

A more moderate version of the distributionist position concentrates on the number of vacant dwellings. But, while absolute numbers of vacant dwellings always appear large, their proportion of the total dwelling stock is one of the lowest in Europe at 3.4 per cent (Eurostat, 2010). No country manages to go much below that, because there are always transitory vacancies.

There is only one statistic on which the UK is clearly an international outlier, and that is the completion rate of new dwellings over time, which is illustrated in Figure 3. The figure does not include countries such as Ireland and Spain, which have experienced construction bubbles and now have very low completion rates. But, even so, the contrast between the UK and its neighbouring countries remains stark. UK completion rates show much less year-on-year variation, and a much lower long-term average. Many countries have displayed low completion rates at some point in time. But no other country has suppressed residential development with such rigour for so long.

What is most astonishing is that completion rates remained

Figure 3   Dwellings completed per 10,000 inhabitants, north-western Europe

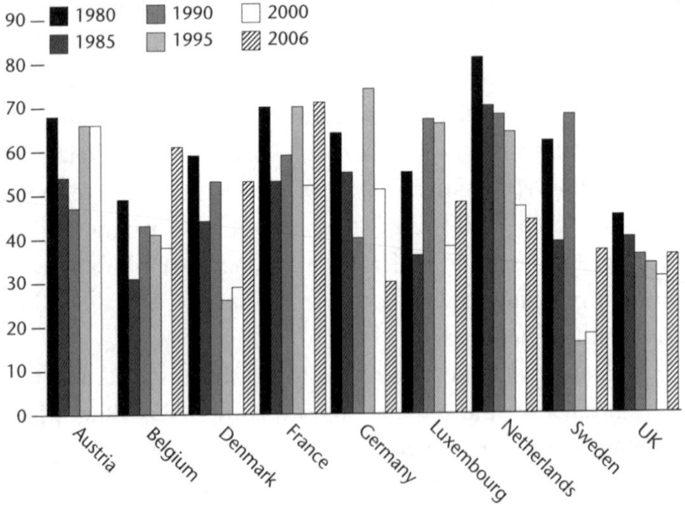

Note: Data for 2005 not available; data for Austria only available up to 2000.
Sources: Based on data from Eurostat (2010: 74) and ONS & DCLG (2012)

perfectly flat during the most intense phase of the house price explosion (Oxley et al., 2009: 62). Housing supply in the UK has become completely unresponsive to demand.

What should be done?

In a restrictive planning system, planning authorities *can* easily block development, but this does not, in itself, explain why they actually do so. This only becomes understandable when recognising how poorly the costs and benefits of development are aligned in the current framework (see Pennington, 2002: 61–7). For a local community, new development entails only negative aspects: noise and nuisance; a loss of green fields; more traffic congestion; crowding; and, for homeowners, a decline in the value of their house. Through 'Section 106' payments, developers compensate local authorities in a somewhat roundabout way for explicit monetary costs they cause, but not for the aforementioned disadvantages. Development also generates benefits, but these do not accrue to local residents. There are at least two benefits worthy of mention:

- When planning permission is granted, the value of a piece of land multiplies, or indeed explodes in some regions. But the vast majority of residents do not benefit from this increase, which accrues to the owner and/or the developer. As Leunig (2007: 17) explains: 'In the South East of England, for example, agricultural land is worth £7,410 per hectare, with residential land worth £3.32 million. The owner of an average sized 57 hectare farm could thus make a windfall gain of £189 million from development.' The gain is subject to taxation, but 'none of it accrues directly to the local authority' (or indeed to local residents, one might add).
- Up to a point, there are economies of scale in the use of public services. New development broadens the taxpayer base, which should enable either a lowering of local tax rates, or an improvement of local public services (or a combination of both). But owing to the high level of centralisation in the current tax system, such considerations play no role in the local decision-making process.

In both cases, the reason why these gains are more or less irrelevant at the local level is that fiscal autonomy of sub-national levels of government is virtually non-existent in the UK. Ninety-five per cent of all tax revenue accrues to the central government, a share which is even higher than in France (87 per cent), which has traditionally been regarded as a textbook model of centralised governance. In federal systems such as those of the USA, Switzerland and Germany, the federal governments receive less than 70 per cent of the total tax take (OECD, 2011b).

The great inconsistency in the current set-up is that the planning system is partially localised, while the tax system is heavily centralised: both competencies should be held at the same level, either both fully centralised or both fully localised. This is an either-or. Combinations are not sensible.

There is a strong argument for the preferable option being full localism. Localism has been found to improve accountability and efficiency in public services provision, and a composition of public services which matches voters' preferences more closely (Blankart, 2007, 2008; Feld et al., 2004). But this would require a complete overhaul of the fiscal architecture and of local governance. It also means that many more policy areas should be devolved to the local level. A strong candidate for this is welfare, which will be explored in greater detail in Chapter 9.

Local authorities should become largely self-funding, with full control over their tax systems, as well as the composition, level and quality of local public services. Revenue would be raised from, for example, a local income tax and a local land value tax, which can show huge variations across the country. In such a system, planning decisions could be left exclusively to local authorities, rather than spread across various layers of government as in the current system. Local decision-makers would be free to be as permissive or restrictive as they see fit. As a rule of thumb, the more permissive their approach to planning, the larger the local tax base they would generate so that taxes would reduce for residents.

Anti-development groups such as CPRE are aware of this, which is why they oppose localism:

> By permitting new development councils would be widening their tax base and ultimately increasing their tax revenues. [...] No doubt such a reform would soon deliver tracts of low density, detached housing stretching far out into the countryside from today's urban edges. But most people do not want the Green Belts around our towns and cities looking like the San Fernando Valley or other parts of Greater Los Angeles. (CPRE, 2006: 20)

But this is a bizarre logic, because a fully localised system would be much more responsive to local preferences than the current one. It would not rule out nimbyism, but it would make the opportunity cost of nimbyism more visible. Signing a petition, joining a citizen's initiative, participating in a town hall meeting or expressing an opinion in a survey is one thing. Knowingly waiving lower local taxes and/or more/better local public services is another. A localised system would enable rational trade-offs between various goals, which are all desirable, but which are also in conflict with one another. Hence the hostility of CPRE to localism and the freedom of choice it implies: it is extremely unlikely that when making informed trade-offs, and facing the consequences of their choices, people would take the extreme anti-development stance of CPRE. And this is precisely what makes full localisation a promising way out of the housing afford-ability crisis.

In the longer run, planning should be removed from the political sphere entirely, by converting development rights into freely tradable private property titles (Pennington, 2002; Corkindale, 2004). Indeed, even in the short run it should be possible to develop some system of compensation for those whose environmental amenities were affected by development. This would give maximum scope to the discovery-process function of markets, whereby completely different systems for determining and governing land use could coexist side by side.

Reforming planning is arguably the most important ingredient in a market-based anti-poverty strategy. There would be large direct effects but, in addition, slashing housing costs would benefit low earners in many additional ways, such as by producing lower retail prices and stronger work incentives (arising from the reduction in housing benefit and the taxes necessary to finance it). Planning liberalisation is not a poverty 'silver bullet', but it is the closest to one that a policy measure can get. No poverty campaigner can be regarded as taking poverty seriously unless they take this issue into account.

4 CHILDCARE

Childcare costs on the rise

The Daycare Trust's annual childcare costs surveys have been documenting sharp above-inflation increases in the cost of child-care for a number of years in a row. According to the latest survey (Daycare Trust, 2012), the average annual cost of a part-time nursery place for a young child has now risen to over £5,000. Expressed as an hourly rate, this corresponds to two-thirds of the national minimum wage. If they were not heavily subsidised, childcare services would now be a luxury good.

This can be seen by looking at the childcare costs of families that rely on childcare services, but which no longer qualify for large subsidies. For a two-earner household, where one partner earns the average wage and the other earns half the average wage, childcare costs absorb as much as 28 per cent of family income. In an international comparison, this figure is not unique – in Ireland and the USA the position is similar. But, nevertheless, the costs are atypically high (OECD, 2011a).

This result is not due to a lack of public spending. There is a complex array of instruments to support families with childcare costs: benefits in cash and in kind; means-tested and universal, work-contingent and age-contingent benefits; and so on. The childcare element of the working tax credit refunds 70 per

Table 17 **Childcare, costs and outcomes compared**

	Public expenditure on childcare services, % of GDP	Out-of-pocket cost of childcare as a % of income*
Ireland	0.3	31
Austria	0.3	15
South Korea	0.3	11
Japan	0.3	17
Luxembourg	0.4	5
Portugal	0.4	4
USA	0.4	30
Australia	0.4	13
Germany	0.4	14
Spain	0.5	6
Italy	0.6	n/a
Netherlands	0.7	9
New Zealand	0.8	4
Belgium	0.8	4
Iceland	0.9	6
Finland	0.9	10
Norway	1.0	14
France	1.0	9
UK	1.1	28
Sweden	1.1	6
Denmark	1.3	11

*Assumes a two-earner household where one partner earns the average wage and the other partner half the average wage.
Source: Based on data from OECD (2011a: 141–4, 167–69)

cent of childcare costs, subject to a cap. Under the 'Early Years' programme, three- and four-year-olds are entitled to fifteen hours of free nursery schooling per week. Sure Start Children's Centres offer a variety of child-related services, typically including childcare at subsidised rates. There are also programmes which incentivise employers to provide, contract or co-finance childcare for their employees, for example through tax-deductible childcare vouchers.

Taken together, public expenditure on childcare through all these different channels has increased massively since 1997, trebling in real terms over the course of a decade (Stewart et al., 2009: 52). As a proportion of GDP, it has risen to one of the highest levels in the world, now being on a par with that of Sweden and well ahead of those of most of western Europe – see Table 17.

This leaves many British parents in a position where they have to pay high childcare costs twice, first in their role as taxpayers and then again in their role as service users. The above is a crude comparison of aggregates, which does not take account of differences in service quality, demographics, employment patterns or other relevant variables. But it nevertheless indicates serious flaws in the model of childcare provision.

Why does it matter?

Childcare services are not just purchased for convenience, but can be instrumental to parents entering the labour market and earning a wage. This was one of the key arguments behind the massive expansion of public spending on childcare. During the last Labour government, real-terms spending on childcare subsidies was increased by about 12 per cent per annum, as part of a strategy to raise work levels among low-income parents. Lack of affordable childcare was assumed to be one of the key barriers to work, especially for single parents (see Brewer and Shephard, 2004: 3–4). It is very likely that this strategy was based on overestimation of the importance of childcare in providing a route into work (see

Morgan, 2007: 31), but there was nevertheless some truth in the general reasoning. For those who do not have informal means of childcare, the cost of formal provision is a work-related cost, no different in principle from the cost of commuting or of purchasing suitable work attire. Rising childcare costs reduce the pay-off from entering work, and from progressing in the labour market.

As long as childcare is as expensive as it currently is, however, it is doubtful whether the aim of making it readily accessible to low earners is a realistic one. So far, despite the huge and sustained increases in public spending, results have not been especially impressive. The UK has reached Nordic levels of public childcare *expenditure*, but it does not come near Nordic levels of coverage among low earners (see Table 18). About a quarter of low-income families use formal childcare services, roughly the same proportion as much of continental Europe attains at a fraction of the cost.

Again, this is a comparison of crude aggregates with no information on other relevant factors, so one should not read too much into the figures. But they do point to the shortcomings of a strategy that ignores the causes of the cost escalation, and attempts to whitewash the consequences through continual increases in spending.

Even where this model does provide access, there are problems with using subsidies as a substitute for affordable market prices. Means-tested subsidies have to be withdrawn at some point, exposing recipients to taper rates. This drawback has been highlighted in the previous chapter for the case of housing benefit, which has also increasingly been used as a substitute for affordable rents. The same logic applies to the childcare element of working tax credit, which is received by 0.5 million households.

Table 18 **Childcare enrolment rate among low-income families**

Denmark	72%
Iceland	58%
Sweden	49%
Norway	42%
Netherlands	40%
Luxembourg	31%
Belgium	30%
Portugal	28%
United Kingdom	27%
Italy	25%
Germany	23%
Spain	23%
Finland	15%
Austria	12%
Ireland	9%
Greece	8%

Source: Based on data from OECD (2011a)

If fully used,[1] this amounts to about £500 per month for one child, and £900 for two or more children, which means that it can represent up to half a family's total tax credit entitlement. Through the childcare element, tax credit payments are linked to the cost of childcare. When the cost of childcare rises, more people become eligible. Therefore, high childcare costs inevitably weaken work incentives even when subsidies keep childcare affordable, because they expose more people to the withdrawal rate.

Table 19 below illustrates this for two household types, a two-earner couple with two children and a single parent with one

---

1   Not many recipients use the full amount, because half of them work between 16 and 24 hours a week, and thus cannot claim childcare cost refunds for more hours than that.

child. For both household types, two scenarios are shown: one in which formal childcare is required and one in which it is not. The bottom line shows the gross income up to which these households qualify for tax credits: the income level at which tax credits have been fully tapered away.

Table 19 shows that the single parent not requiring childcare services would receive tax credits as long as their income does not exceed £25,700. If their income crosses this threshold, their effective marginal tax rate falls from 73 per cent to 32 per cent. With childcare, however, the threshold moves up to £41,200, greatly lengthening the income range over which the effective marginal tax rate of 73 per cent applies. For the family of four, the distance between the two thresholds is even greater.

Table 19 **The impact of childcare costs on work incentives**

	Two adults, both in work, two pre-school children		Single parent, in work, one pre-school child	
Formal childcare required:	no	yes	no	yes
Total working tax credit (WTC) entitlement	£10,600	£21,500*	£7,900	£14,250†
Out of which childcare element	£0	£10,900	£0	£6,350
Gross income at which WTC/ CTC expires	£32,250	£58,850§	£25,700	£41,200

* Basic element of WTC + Couple element of WTC + 30 hours element of WTC + Family element of CTC + 2 x Child element of CTC = £1,920 + £1,950 + £790 + £545 + 2 × £2,690 = £10,585.

† Basic element of WTC + Lone parent element of WTC + 30 hours element of WTC + Family element of CTC + Child element of CTC = £1,920 + £1,950 + £790 + £545 + £2,690 = £7,895.

§ (Total entitlement/Taper rate) + Threshold = (£21,505/0.41) + £6,420 = £58,871.

What this table shows is a comparison of extreme cases. In reality, it is more typical for working tax credit recipient families to fall somewhere in between, receiving some childcare payments but not the full amount. But it is nevertheless true that, other things being equal, any reduction in childcare costs takes some families out of the tax credit taper, simply because they can now afford the same amount of childcare at lower market rates so they receive less benefit and this benefit does not have to be tapered away. Affordable childcare at market prices is desirable both for its static and for its dynamic effects.

A secondary effect – as with housing benefit, in fact – is that the childcare element of tax credits has to be financed by taxes. The higher the level of spending on these tax credits, the higher taxes have to be. Depending on how taxes are adjusted at the margin to finance tax credits, some group will have worsened work incentives when spending on tax credits is increased.

What is going wrong?

Poverty campaigners have long criticised the patchy coverage among low earners (CPAG, 2008: 32, 36–7). But since they completely ignore the question of why childcare costs are so high in the first place, their recommendations are rather predictable. CPAG, characteristically, criticises the linking of childcare subsidies to work, arguing that

> targeting financial support via working tax credit reinforces the message that childcare is primarily designed to enable parents to work and has resulted in systems that may exclude the most disadvantaged children whose parents are not in work. (Ibid.)

Their conclusion is that childcare should be provided unconditionally, universally and free at the point of use. This is a superficial conclusion. The further removal of conditions would necessarily lead to an explosion in demand, forcing providers to revert to more tacit forms of rationing. There is no convincing alternative to a competitive market structure, in which childcare is easily affordable at market rates to the vast majority of people. This requires addressing the cost drivers directly.

The area of childcare provision is an ideal example of the type of policy mix that is being criticised throughout this monograph: policymakers have simultaneously driven up the cost of this service, while also increasing transfers to offset the consequences. Since the late 1990s, childcare has become an increasingly standardised, uniform profession (see Shackleton, 2011: 113–16). The government now sets detailed requirements about staff qualifications, staff-to-children ratios, conditions of the premises, safety measures, activities, etc. The understandable motivation was to even out gaps in pre-school education between children from different socio-economic backgrounds. But while this objective could justify an earmarked subsidy to poor parents, it is not clear why it should require a regulation of inputs, processes and industry structure. It is clear that each of these regulatory standards imposes costs on the sector. This begins at market entry, as Truss (2012) explains: 'In order to be a childminder, applicants must apply to Ofsted for approval, a process which takes 4–6 months and which after paying for registration and training costs around £400 for each childminder.'

Regulatory standards and selective subsidies have also profoundly altered the industry structure, because they generally favour nurseries over independent childminders. As a result, the composition of childcare provision has shifted heavily towards the former. Until the late 1990s, the ratio of nursery places to places with childminders was about 1:2, a ratio which has more than reversed since then (ibid.: 2). This structure may be politically favoured, but it does not seem to be a cost-effective one.

Among the set of input regulations, one that is especially note-worthy is the mandatory maximum children-to-staff ratio, which is 3:1 for children aged one to five and 1:1 for those younger than one (ibid.: 7). There are no estimates of the extent to which this raises the cost of provision, but in any sector characterised by high fixed costs, the ability to spread these is crucial.

What should be done?

Some markets have been characterised by a high level of state involvement for such a long time that the case for deregulation needs to be made in great detail. This is the case because the question of what a deregulated market would look like is a very hypothetical one. Childcare is not such a case. The current level of state regulation is a fairly recent phenomenon. This less formal model which existed until the late 1990s was not abandoned because of its failures. Rather, the Labour government was caught between two conflicting objectives: it was trying to make childcare more affordable while also trying to turn it into an instrument for social engineering. The first objective has been torpedoed by the cost increase which resulted from pursuing the second objective. The present coalition seems set to continue the same trajectory of increased formalisation through regulation. The interim version of the Nutbrown Review (Nutbrown, 2012) has recently criticised shortcomings in the quality of childcare, and proposed, among other things, higher requirements for the formal qualifications of childcare staff.

The coalition should do the precise opposite. Childcare should be deregulated – but it is important to note that the alternative to statutory regulation is not 'no regulation'. Rather, there is a conflicting relationship between statutory and private forms of regulation.[2] In markets where consumers demand quality signals about a product that they cannot easily judge for themselves, suppliers are enticed to look for signalling devices. In the case of childcare, it could fall on childminding agencies to devise standards that their members must meet, and rules they must follow.[3] The fact that a particular childcare provider belongs to such an agency would be an easy public demonstration of their quality. If the case for government intervention is seen in informational asymmetries, it would be more logical to argue for very specific interventions addressing these asymmetries directly, rather than having a regime of general government regulation. For example, childcare providers could be legally required to disclose selected pieces of information, which could also be collected and publicised by the government.[4] What the government should not be involved with is the day-to-day business of childcare provision. It should not regulate inputs, least of all specific inputs such as staff ratios. Needless to say, this approach

---

2   Arthur and Booth (2010) discuss this relationship with regard to financial markets, but identify general principles that can apply to any market.

3   See Truss (2012: 5–6) on the role of childminding agencies in the Netherlands, albeit within a wider framework of government regulation.

4   This form of regulation does have dangers and is inferior to some kind of 'badging' or approval process by a private entity. If selected pieces of information have to be given to the public, there is then a temptation for the childcare provider to orientate their business model towards these metrics to too great an extent.

is easily compatible with the toughest stance on fraud, abuse and breach of contract.

The funding streams for childcare need to be merged and greatly simplified. There is no reason for employing more than one instrument for one objective. Among the current set of instruments, the most sensible funding stream is the childcare element of the working tax credit for the following reasons:

- Parents are free to use the childcare element for any childcare provider they choose, so funding is entirely demand-driven.
- There is a 30 per cent co-payment so that parents retain an incentive to seek value for money.
- It is integrated into working tax credit and so is relatively well targeted at low earners.
- Working tax credit is work-contingent, ensuring that the childcare element of working tax credit is also.

A single payment along these lines should replace all others, providing a limited subject subsidy in an environment in which most parents find childcare affordable on an unsubsidised basis.

5 FOOD

Food prices on the rise

In 1977, an average British household still had to reserve 25 per cent of its budget for food and (non-alcoholic) drinks. In 2010, households in the second-lowest decile of the income distribution reserved 17 per cent for this item, and households in the bottom decile 15 per cent. Today's least well off spend relatively less on food than the middle classes a generation earlier. This is the combined result of rising incomes and a long-term decrease in the relative price of food. Taking a long-term perspective, this is a success story, especially when bearing in mind how the quality and variety of food have also improved.

But when considering a more recent period, the picture is mixed. From 2005 onwards, food prices have shown steep increases, catapulting the topic back into the news headlines. Between 2005 and the end of 2011, while the overall consumer price level increased by about one fifth, food prices increased by more than one third (ONS, 2011a).

While food expenditure as a proportion of the expenditure of low earners is at a historic low today, the same was already true a decade earlier (ONS, 2003). The progress that has been made on this front has been made in the past; it has not been built upon for at least a decade, and there has even been a partial reversal.

Figure 4   **Food prices and the CPI since 2000**

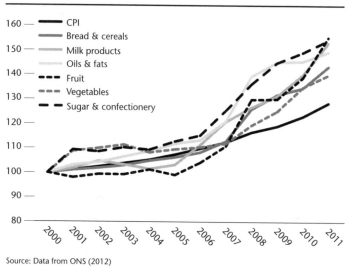

Source: Data from ONS (2012)

Several sources, including the OECD and Chatham House, expect food prices to remain on their current high plateau in real terms for the foreseeable future, not least because of a slowdown in agricultural productivity growth (Rickard, 2012: 6–12).

Why is it a problem?

For households in the lower third of the income distribution,[1] expenditure on food constitutes 15–17 per cent of their total budget, compared with a population average of 11 per cent.

---

1   Ordered by gross equivalised income.

Changes in food prices have a much larger impact on low-income households than their impact on the overall CPI would suggest. The CPI is based on the consumption behaviour of average households, not of low-income households, which can effectively experience a very different inflation rate.

The debate on the relationship between income, eating habits and health is a contentious one, and far beyond the scope of this monograph to explore. But it is safe to say that while it is entirely *possible* to adhere to a healthy diet on a low income, it is certainly *easier* to do so when food prices are generally low, and when such a diet can include more and tastier options.

High food prices, if they persist, also make income replacement benefits at a higher level necessary. This relationship is not nearly as straightforward as in the case of housing benefit and the working tax credit childcare element, which are explicitly and automatically linked to the cost of housing and childcare, respectively. There is no such link between food prices and the rates of income support or jobseekers' allowance; however, it is difficult to imagine that the former have no impact whatsoever on the latter over time. So, there is a case for focusing on food prices both in a static and in a dynamic perspective.

What is going wrong?

The increase in food prices has very little in common with the price increases in other sectors discussed elsewhere in this monograph. It is not a UK-specific phenomenon; it is not caused by any recent policy changes; and there is no obvious single factor which could account for most of it. To a large extent, it is caused by global drivers which are out of the control of domestic policymakers.

Therefore, this chapter will not deal with the specific causes of the recent surge in food prices. The latter will merely be taken as an occasion for reviewing the permanent, structural inflators built into agricultural policies. These inflators, namely tariffs, non-tariff trade barriers and distorting domestic subsidies, have existed from well before the current price surge. They may have been more tolerable in times when they were outweighed by countervailing factors, but they are arguably less tolerable now that food prices are rising.

The general economic case against protectionism is theoretically and empirically so well established that it needs no repetition here. Economists may agree on little else, but free trade is one of the areas where a broad consensus exists across completely different schools of economic thought. In a survey among members of the American Economic Association, 83 per cent agreed with the statement 'The US should eliminate remaining tariffs and other barriers to trade', while only 10 per cent disagreed (Whaples, 2009: 340). And while the politics of the day may often be impervious to economic advice, the last decades have been characterised by a general tendency towards freer trade in most sectors (see World Bank, 2011b). A remarkable example is the Agreement on Textiles and Clothing (ATC), the roadmap for the phasing out of EU textile quotas between 1995 and 2005. Although completion was effectively delayed until 2009 (European Commission, n.d.), the ATC has led to a staged opening of the European textile market, which had long been used to high levels of protection. The liberalisation has greatly benefited consumers, particularly low earners. Between 1996 and 2005, prices for clothing and footwear in the UK fell in real terms by nearly one half (Francois et al., 2007: 11–14). It has been shown that the fall in the price of clothing arose as a result of the dismantling of trade barriers. Statistical analysis has been made easier because quotas for different types of clothes were lifted at different times (ibid.: 22–5). The benefits to consumers are still accruing: between 2005 and 2011, despite high overall inflation, clothing and footwear prices fell, even in nominal terms (ONS, 2011a).

But while the opening of markets has, at long last, been a success story in the textile industry, agriculture has remained a bastion of protectionism and distorting subsidies. The stubborn persistence of agricultural protection sometimes irritates economists, because the case for free trade in agriculture is no less clear cut than in other sectors:

> [M]ost economists are quick to point out [that] the costs of protecting the agricultural sector in the developed countries clearly outweigh the benefits to these societies as a whole. [...] Agricultural exceptionalism in the developed world is therefore an inefficient curiosity for economists. (Thies and Porche, 2007: 116)

Indeed, much of the more recent empirical literature has not been about *whether* agricultural protection causes a net welfare loss, but about the relative contribution of trade barriers and domestic subsidies to the welfare loss (e.g. Anderson et al., 2006; Hoekman et al., 2004). The finding that removal of agricultural protection would cause a net welfare gain, even in a static perspective, is only reconfirmed in passing.

The impact of interventions into agricultural markets is obscured by their sheer multitude. Apart from a complex array of tariffs and quotas, there are literally hundreds of policy instruments to support agricultural producers (see OECD, 2010a,

2010b, for an overview). There are different subsidies for different types of agricultural outputs, for different types of agricultural inputs, for different types of capital goods, and for different types of production-related services. There are subsidies based on the total farmland area, subsidies based on the farmland area currently under cultivation, subsidies based on livestock, subsidies based on the farm's revenue, and subsidies based on farmers' income. All of these can be further subdivided according to the specific conditions attached to them. Agricultural support has, to say the least, reached a high level of complexity.

OECD.StatExtracts (2012), however, provides summary estimates of these measures' net effects on producers, taxpayers and consumers. The net transfer from consumers to producers is captured by the ratio of domestic prices to world market prices, recorded at the border. Prices are collected at the farm-gate level, in order to control for variations unrelated to agricultural policy, such as the structure of the retail sector or the tax system. On this basis, European food prices have, on average, been 11 per cent above world market levels in the 2005–10 period. In interpreting this figure, it must be borne in mind that many support measures are countercyclical, in the sense that they are inversely related to world market prices. Since the latter were atypically high over the period, the level of redistribution from consumers to farmers has been atypically low. Averaged over the 2000–10 period, the mark-up was 17 per cent. It was 22 per cent averaged over the 1995–2010 period, and 28 per cent for 1990–2010.

This is a crude measure because it assumes a uniform food consumption pattern across Europe, so the price mark-up paid by low earners in the UK could have been above or below these values. Still, given the limited income and price elasticity of food consumption, it is not unreasonable to interpret this figure as indicative of the cost of the Common Agricultural Policy (CAP) to consumers across the board. Given the share of food expenditure in low earners' budgets, this means the cost of the Common Agricultural Policy represents 2–3 per cent of their annual expenditure, and more for larger families. This is a lower bound: it only shows how much low earners pay in their role as consumers, ignoring any payments they make in their role as taxpayers. On the whole, state support measures account for 25 per cent of European farmers' revenue (averaged over the 2005–10 period).

This shows that, even in a purely static perspective, a removal of agricultural protection would have an immediate and measurable impact on low earners' living standards. Why, then, is a phasing out of the CAP not even on the European agenda, when liberalisation worked so well in the textile sector?

Why agriculture?

Public choice economics can explain reasonably well why agriculture has become one of the most protected and most state-dependent parts of the economy. In principle, *every* sector has an interest in some measure of state protection, but there is wide variation in the extent to which different sectors clamour for it. This is because protection does not come for free; it is a function of costly lobbying efforts. In public choice models, market actors are often assumed to regard lobbying as an investment like any other: every pound invested in political favour-seeking can no longer be invested in productive economic activities. So long as the latter provide a higher return than the former, market actors will concentrate more on running their actual business than on engaging in politics. Yet in agriculture, there are a number of conditions that make large-scale investment in the political market especially lucrative (see Nedergard, 2006; Thies and Porche, 2007).

Demand for agricultural products is characterised by low income and price elasticities, the scope for product innovation and product differentiation is limited, and the number of (potential) competitors is large. Meanwhile, farmers' political interests are sufficiently homogeneous, and farmers' associations with high affiliation rates and large endowment funds (sometimes created with public assistance) already exist. This makes it easier to overcome free-rider problems (the phenomenon that favourable legislation benefits a sector as a whole rather than just the firms that fund the lobbying activities). It also enables peer pressure to discourage potential dissenters. On top of this, the fact that agricultural subsidies tend to be capitalised into the value of land mobilises another powerful interest group: landowners, whose political clout has already been discussed in Chapter 3. In short, there is strong and effective political demand for protection.

The fact that the policy is centralised at the European Union level exacerbates the problem, and so does the fact that it is devolved to a specialist bureaucracy rather than handled by elected representatives.[2] This bureaucracy has an interest in maintaining and strengthening its own position, and the policy's level of complexity is conducive to this aim. Resistance to the policy from those who shoulder its cost – consumers

---

2   There may be other issues related to the EU involvement that make this issue more difficult to solve – not least the majorities needed within the voting system to turn back legislation.

and taxpayers – is not to be expected. The costs and benefits of lobbying to these groups are dispersed, opaque and difficult to assess. The affected groups are too large and heterogeneous to organise as a political lobby. The only group that could be expected to take up that role of a political voice for low-income consumers is the anti-poverty lobby. But poverty campaigners do not concern themselves with such issues; when food prices go up, they call for higher benefits.

What should be done?

None of the above means that market-based agricultural reform is impossible. There are not many reform models, but the ones that exist show one thing: countries that have slashed agricultural protection once have not brought it back in again. The 'yo-yo effect' which characterises many other areas of social spending and subsidisation has so far been absent in agricultural policy. Agricultural reform requires a one-off effort (even though 'one-off' can refer to a period of many years), but not a permanent political commitment. The CAP is one of those policies that would not be introduced today if it did not already exist. It is a settlement born out of the pro-planning mindset that characterised the immediate post-war decades, but it has not died with that mindset because of the inertia it developed in the meantime.

The most frequently cited example of agricultural reform is New Zealand, where the sector was rapidly liberalised while state support was withdrawn. Between 1983 and 1989, agricultural subsidies were cut from 3.8 per cent of GDP to 0.4 per cent. The total value of producer support, which also includes protectionism, fell from 33 per cent of farm revenues to 5 per cent (Sandrey and Scobie, 1994: 1044).[3] Subsequently, the sector underwent a difficult period of restructuring and readjustment, but it then managed to achieve strong productivity growth, both in relation to its own past record and to the overall economy (see Evans and Grimes, 1996; Kalaitzandonakes, 1994; Sandrey & Scobie, 1994).

The fact that New Zealand's farmers have adapted so well to the removal of state support is remarkable, because the sequence of economic reforms was unduly biased against them. Agriculture was the starting point of the reform programme that would become known as 'Rogernomics', and key reforms in this sector preceded those in other areas (Evans and Grimes, 1996: 1859). This meant that farmers found themselves, for a while, in the worst of both worlds: they could no longer count on state support, but they were not yet able to benefit from liberalisations occurring elsewhere in the economy, or from the more stable macroeconomic environment which would eventually result. And yet they did manage to become self-supporting under market conditions, by introducing technological and organisational improvements, and by shifting to more competitive lines within agriculture. The ascent of New Zealand's successful horticulture and wine industries has been linked to the removal of state support (ibid.: 1890–93). Today, New Zealand still has one of the largest agricultural sectors in the developed world, even though producer support accounts for no more than 1 per cent of farm receipts, and farmgate food prices have moved close to world market prices. Since

---

3   The high speed of reform was part of a deliberate strategy, as Finance Minister Roger Douglas later explained: 'Do not try and advance a step at a time. Define your objectives clearly and move towards them in quantum leaps. Otherwise the interest groups will have time to mobilise and drag you down' (quoted in Goldfinch, 2000: 201).

the late 1980s, the price mark-up paid by domestic consumers has never exceeded 4 per cent.

Australia provides another showcase for a largely self-supporting agricultural sector, which thrives with a very low level of protection and subsidies. This case study is less well researched, presumably because the policy shift was less radical. Australian farmers never experienced shock therapy comparable with that experienced by farmers in New Zealand, because the country had never gone the 'European way' of making its farming sector completely state-dependent.

In recent decades, state support measures have gradually fallen from a medium level to a low level, namely from 13 per cent of farm revenues in 1986 to the present level of around 4 per cent. The changes were, however, fairly drastic for individual industries within the sector, and for these the pattern looks similar to the New Zealand experience. Dairy farming had been heavily reliant on subsidies and favourable legislation until the 1980s. When these support measures were gradually withdrawn, the industry went through a difficult period of rationalisation and restructuring, but it then re-emerged as a growth industry (Hogan et al., 2004). What is particularly interesting about the Australian reforms is the almost complete disappearance of direct measures of market price support. Over the past decade, farm-gate prices in Australia have been virtually identical to world market prices in every single year. In this regard, reforms have gone even further than in New Zealand, where small price mark-ups relative to world market prices still remain. Australian farmers still receive some support from taxpayers, but next to none from consumers.[4]

---

4 Support from consumers can be thought of in terms of regulation (for example, restricting imports) that leads to consumer prices for purchases from domestic

As in the case of New Zealand, the agricultural sector remains one of the largest in the developed world.

Finally, Chile provides another, though arguably less comparable, example of a move away from agricultural protectionism and subsidisation. Agriculture in Chile had traditionally been characterised by a high degree of state involvement. Even during the comprehensive economic liberalisation carried out under the military government, agriculture was partially spared (Kurtz, 1999; Errazuriz and Muchnik, 1996). But liberalisation of the sector continued after the transition to democracy, and, in the early 2000s, the level of agricultural protection was finally brought into line with the much lower level in manufacturing (Becerra, 2006). Agriculture nevertheless prospered, shrinking only in relative terms as the economy went through a modernisation phase.

Admittedly, the number of case studies is small, and none of them is exactly transferrable to a European context. In all three examples, climatic conditions are more favourable to agriculture. The impact of the withdrawal of support was cushioned because producers found a refuge which appears almost obvious in hindsight: viticulture (an option which would not be open to British farmers if they had to cope without state support). Also, agricultural reform in the UK is complicated by the fact that this policy area is centralised at the EU level. It is beyond the scope of this monograph to assess whether reform is best pursued in cooperation with other EU member states, or by seeking a repatriation of the relevant responsibilities.

But the general lesson from the above examples is that

producers being higher than world prices. Such support is not as visible as tax-payer-provided support.

Table 20 **Different models of agriculture**

		EU-27	New Zealand	Australia	Chile
Value of producer support measures in % of farm revenues	2005–10	25%	1%	4%	4%
	2000–10	28%	1%	4%	6%
Food price mark-up above world market prices	2005–10	+11%	+2%	+0%	+2%
	2000–10	+17%	+2%	+0%	+5%
Total value of agricultural support (% of GDP)	2005–10	0.9%	0.2%	0.2%	0.4%
	2000–10	1.0%	0.2%	0.2%	0.5%
Agriculture as a % of GDP	2010/11	1.6%	6.2%	3%	3.7%
Agricultural productivity (100 = EU-27*)	2009	100	153	164	36

Sources: Based on data from OECDStat.Extracts (2012), World Bank (2012b, 2012c)
*Arguably, the EU figure is skewed by the productivity gap between eastern and western Europe. Agricultural productivity for western Europe alone is about the same as in New Zealand.

agriculture can be weaned off state support, and come to terms with market conditions. Consumers benefit through lower food prices, as the gap between domestic and world prices narrows (see Table 20). When the emphasis is on lowering food prices for consumers in order to boost low earners' living standards, then, at first sight, the Australian solution of abolishing market price measures while retaining other forms of support seems the most promising route. This model shifts all the burden of farm support from consumers to taxpayers, so it would enable low-income consumers to buy food under world market conditions, while resistance from producers would be cushioned.

But this is only a second-best solution. Only a wholesale abolition of all agricultural subsidies would produce the full range of dynamic benefits. Subsidies make producers less responsive to market forces, reducing incentives to implement technological and organisational innovation rapidly. In addition, a system of selective subsidies such as the CAP distorts production patterns, because business decisions are now taken with a view to maximising entitlements, rather than on the basis of commercial viability. And, not least, a withdrawal of the state from agricultural policy altogether would enable a relocation of the funds currently invested in lobbying activities towards productive uses which benefit consumers.

It is impossible to predict what a self-supporting, undistorted agricultural sector would look like. Rickard (2012: 12–15) believes, however, that there is currently underutilised potential in the use of economies of scale and of biotechnologies. Use of the latter is stifled by ideologically driven, restrictive legislation in the field of GM products. Thus, the ideal policy combination would be an abolition of agricultural protection and subsidies coupled with an abolition of restrictions.

The agricultural industry would become fully exposed to market forces, but it would also be given the liberty to adapt to them, for example by entering potential new growth markets. Ideally, this combination would produce a win-win situation of a more efficient international division of labour, a modernised domestic agricultural sector, and constantly falling food prices. But even in a pessimistic scenario in which the British farming sector does not adapt well to the changed environment, the main advantage remains: there would be substantially lower food prices for low earners, who would be able to buy on the open market.

As a footnote, it is worth mentioning that action could be taken elsewhere in the world that could substantially lessen the upward pressure on food prices. It is estimated, for example, that between 20 and 40 per cent of food in India rots before reaching markets. This is partly because of the absence of decent infrastructure but also because of regulation of the retail sector. There are other countries with similar problems. In addition, non-tariff barriers reduce the exports of food from poorer countries. This puts pressure on global food prices. Of course, the main benefit from policy changes in such countries in these areas would flow to their domestic consumers, but there would be second-round benefits for poor people in other countries who would benefit from lower world food prices.

6 ENERGY

Energy prices on the rise

Energy prices began to soar from about the mid-2000s onwards. Since 2000, while the overall Consumer Price Index (CPI) has increased by just over a quarter, the price level of electricity and solid fuels has just about doubled and the price level of gas and liquid fuels has almost trebled (ONS, 2012).

These increases have occurred within a reasonably well-functioning market. The programme of privatisation and liberalisation of energy provision, which started in 1990 and was formally completed in 2002, has inspired many similar reforms around the world. It has generally been considered a success in terms of productivity, competition and consumer choice (Newbery, 2006; Joskow, 2008), even though legitimate concerns about incumbents' market power remain (Salies and Waddams Price, 2004).

The increase in energy costs has not been unique to the UK, and it is partly due to factors outside of policymakers' control, as politicians are often keen to emphasise. But while that is clearly true, it should not count as an excuse for policies which inflate the cost of energy even further. To a large extent, changes in energy prices *are* policy induced, even if other factors add to them. This chapter will look at some of those policy-induced changes. It is not a comprehensive analysis of energy provision in general.

Figure 5   **Energy prices versus overall CPI**

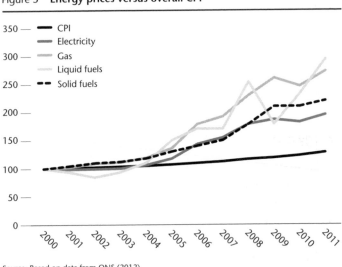

Source: Based on data from ONS (2012)

Why is it a problem?

The concept of 'fuel poverty' is often used to illustrate the impact of fuel prices in one selected area: that of domestic heating. A household is defined to be in fuel poverty when the cost of heating their home to a predefined standard would exceed 10 per cent of their budget, regardless of how much they actually do spend on heating. The concept has been frequently criticised for good reasons. The main downside is not that the thresholds are arbitrary – even though they are – but that it conflates preferences with constraints. If a family with a rather comfortable income chooses to live in a home which is very expensive to heat, but which offers other advantages, it could be considered as being in fuel poverty. But if a family with a low income chooses to live in a small flat in order to avoid high heating costs, they might not be considered fuel poor. This is why the fuel poverty *rate* as such is not informative. It can still be meaningful, however, to look at *changes* in this rate. Even though the above problems still exist, they are unlikely to show much variation in the short term.

The time trend of fuel poverty shows a U-shaped evolution. Between the mid-1990s and the early 2000s, the number of UK households in fuel poverty fell from 6.5 million to just over 2 million. Since then, it has increased to well over 5 million again, undoing much of the progress that had been made before (ONS & DECC, 2011a).

Domestic heating is just one isolated dimension of energy use. There are no similar measures for 'mobility poverty' or 'electricity poverty', and no comprehensive information on how the cost pass-through from energy-intensive industries affects low earners. But it is safe to say that energy costs affect low earners in a variety of ways.

A sizeable share of energy costs, as will be shown below, is due to environmental measures. The most visible among these measures are environmental taxes, which have come to represent about 6 per cent of disposable income for those in the bottom decile of the distribution (based on data from ONS, 2010).[1] The cost of environmental regulation is harder to quantify, but via its impact on product prices, it must have a similarly regressive effect.

The conventional rationale for environmental taxes is the internalisation of externalities. If the world worked like an

---

1   This is the sum of the duty on hydrocarbon oils, vehicle excise duty and air passenger duty.

Economics 101 textbook, every green tax would be equal to the marginal external cost caused by the taxed activity (a Pigouvian tax). For a number of reasons, actual environmental policies cannot come close to the textbook situation. In particular, it is notoriously difficult to assign monetary values to, for example, two different levels of air quality, even from the perspective of a single individual. Doing the same for a heterogeneous population with very different preferences is an impossibility. But for common-pool resources which cannot reasonably be managed outside of the collective sphere, there is probably no alternative to attempting to estimate social costs, and setting Pigouvian taxes accordingly.

Environmental taxes are thus justifiable to the extent that they represent genuine Pigouvian taxes. The fact that they are regressive is lamentable, but not sensibly alterable. But to the extent that environmental taxes exceed an activity's external cost, they cease to be Pigouvian taxes, and can no longer be justified on environmental grounds. They then become either moralistic taxes with the sole purpose of penalising consumption, or just another means of raising revenue. Sinclair (2011: 130–40) shows that the important green taxes in the UK already exceed the available estimates of external costs. They are no longer pure environmental taxes.

The political debate

It is not surprising that environmentalist groups such as Greenpeace and Friends of the Earth do not point this out. Environmentalism has become so inextricably mingled with anti-consumerism that the two are virtually indistinguishable. In the combined environmentalist/anti-consumerist perspective, environmental protection is not about a trade-off, with losses in material living standards being weighed against environmental damage. Enforced reductions in consumption are not presented as a necessary price to pay for fending off environmental disasters, but as virtuous and desirable in their own right.[2]

What is more surprising is that poverty campaigners show no inclination to be a moderating voice in this debate, balancing the environmentalist zeal for costly and regressive policies. The whole area is another blank space in the work of the poverty campaigners. They focus intensely on fuel poverty and surrounding issues, but they are reluctant to address the green policies that are important underlying drivers. Poverty campaigners either avoid the topic altogether, or even try to portray poverty alleviation and carbon reduction as allies.

This tendency is most pronounced among campaigners who are concerned with both global and domestic poverty. Oxfam manages to run campaigns for climate policy measures that would raise fuel bills further (e.g. Cugelmann and Otero, 2010), while simultaneously running campaigns against fuel poverty (e.g. Oxfam, 2009). Part of this evasion strategy is the portrayal of climate change as an injustice that 'the rich' are inflicting on 'the poor'. This is convenient because it presses the issue into a familiar narrative, while keeping the distribution of roles rather vague.

---

2   To be fair, there are thinkers within the environmental movement who criticise this line of thinking. Deben (2012: 32) speaks of the 'more extreme of green campaigners, whose penchant for misery is unbounded. Their puritan belief that we would all be better off colder and less well fed fuels the proposition that a low-carbon future will mean considerable and extensive self-denial.' He still advocates cuts in living standards, but does not claim it is a win-win strategy.

In a global perspective low earners in the UK are 'the rich', even when ignoring the least developed countries. On a purchasing power parity adjusted basis, incomes of the lowest decile in the UK are about twice as high as median incomes in Mexico, and in the neighbourhood of median incomes in Poland, Hungary and Slovakia (based on data from OECD, 2008). More committed environmentalists are fully aware of this. Lord Deben (2012: 33), for example, argues that 'the least well off [in the UK] are rich in the context of the real poor in developing countries'. He proposes a climate policy that distributes the burden 'progressively', but makes no attempt to conceal the fact that it would lower living standards in the developed world across the board.

Thus, there is a whole set of nuances in this debate. Climate change measures might affect the poorest in the world if they reduce development in poor countries. On the other hand, if climate change measures are mainly focused on rich countries (either through unilateral action or through the particular way in which international agreements are drawn up) it is likely to be the less well off in developed countries who suffer the most – even if those people are well off by global standards.

This recognition of distributional costs of climate change measures is rare. Commonly, poverty campaigners avoid criticising environmental measures by simply limiting their work to the few low-hanging-fruit areas, where their aims are compatible with those of environmentalists. There are few such areas. Improving energy efficiency through better home insulation, for example, could address fuel poverty while also reducing emissions – but such measures can only be taken so far. A commitment to low earners' living standards can be compatible with moderate environmental objectives, but not with environmentalism as an ideology. It is for this reason that the more committed environmentalists, who have no illusions about this, attack and ridicule the idea that emissions could be reduced through improved energy efficiency. Wallis (2012: 2) argues: '[W]e are told that we can save the planet simply by changing our light bulbs or insulating our roofs. These things are offered to us as a "win-win": save the planet whilst saving money.' In his view, the major task for environmentalists is 'to alleviate the current dissonance created by the suggestion you can plausibly fend off a pending global catastrophe armed with only a smart meter' (ibid.: 5).

Environmentalists are not opposed to improving energy efficiency, but they see it as only a very minor ingredient in a strategy of reducing emissions. The reason is not pessimism about the technological potential for efficiency improvements. It is an application of the 'Jevons Paradox', the observation that improvements in the efficiency of a resource's usage can increase, rather than decrease, its consumption. This is explained by Wilkinson and Pickett (2009: 223) in *The Spirit Level*:

> Imagine that a new generation of car engines is introduced which halve fuel consumption. Driving would then be cheaper and that would save us money, but it is money which we would almost certainly spend on something else. We might spend it on driving more, or buying a bigger car, or on more power-hungry equipment – perhaps a bigger fridge-freezer. [...] As cars have become more fuel-efficient, we have chosen to drive further. As houses have become better insulated we have raised standards for heating [...] Because energy-saving innovations mean that we can buy more, they are like economic growth.

The authors argue that emissions cannot be reduced by

improving energy efficiency, but only by ending all economic growth in developed countries, and establishing a so-called 'steady state economy' (i.e. a zero-growth economy). In a steady state economy, the government controls economic activity in such a way that the level of output is maintained constant. Wilkinson and Pickett do not specify at what precise level of economic output they want to 'freeze' the British economy, but it follows that it would be at a level substantially below the current one:

> Carbon emissions per head in rich countries are between two and five times higher than the world average. But cutting their emissions by a half or four fifths will not be enough: world totals are already too high and allowances must be made for economic growth in poorer countries. (Ibid.: 217)

Not everybody committed to 'decarbonising' the economy would go as far as these authors. Most would advocate some combination of reduced living standards and increased energy efficiency. But what one cannot sensibly claim is that the aims of reducing emissions and raising low earners' living standards go hand in hand. Environmentalists may be willing to make these trade-offs – even if they tend to prefer not to mention them explicitly. This is not surprising. What is surprising is that poverty campaigners seem to be unaware of the trade-offs between raising the living standards of the poor and the pursuit of a low-carbon economy.

What is going wrong?

Green policies are very complex and it is impossible to go beyond scratching the surface here. But it is possible to single out one policy area which suffers from a particular lack of consistency, leading to unnecessarily high costs with a regressive incidence: the subsidisation of renewable energy.

Under the Renewables Obligation (RO) scheme and related provisions, such as mandatory feed-in tariffs (FiTs), energy retailers are legally required to purchase ever-increasing shares of their portfolio from renewable sources. The additional cost is passed on to consumers via household energy bills. So, technically speaking, the RO and FiTs are neither green taxes nor taxpayer-funded subsidies. But they work, to all intents and purposes, like a subsidy for renewable energy providers financed through a green tax on energy consumers. RO/FiTs are accompanied by other schemes aimed at discouraging the consumption of energy from conventional sources. The combined cost of these policies is shown in the table below, expressed as a percentage of total retail energy prices. They represent DECC forecasts for 2015, but most of the measures driving them are already in effect. The cost of these measures is also included in the denominator, so the figures show by how much gas and electricity prices would drop if the measures were abolished (and not by how much they raise market prices).

Given current expenditure patterns for gas and electricity, this means that, by 2015, renewable energy subsidies and related measures will cost households in the bottom income decile more than 1 per cent of their annual budgets. Additional measures are scheduled for the years after 2015, leading to yet sharper increases.

These figures do not show the complete picture. Energy bills are a product of unit prices and quantities consumed, and the above-mentioned measures are accompanied by subsidy programmes to increase the energy efficiency of British homes.

Table 21 **The cost of subsidies for renewable energies and related measures, as percentage of energy prices, 2015**

	Measures included	Cost in % of domestic retail price
Gas	Future Supplier Obligation, Smart metering Renewable heat incentive	10
Electricity	Renewables Obligation Future Supplier Obligation Smart metering, Carbon capture and storage Feed-in tariffs	16

Source: Based on data from DECC (2010)

According to the DECC's estimates, the combined impact on energy *bills* as opposed to prices will be negligible. As the Joseph Rowntree Foundation (2010) shows, however, the households which will be most adversely affected by the increase in prices are also those least likely to benefit from energy efficiency upgrade measures. In a worst-case scenario, the least well-off households could end up cross-subsidising the better-off, by co-financing the latter's home insulation through their energy bills. The precise distributional impact of the measures remains to be seen; it will depend on the take-up rates of the energy efficiency upgrade subsidies and their effectiveness. But it is already safe to say that while not *all* households in the bottom deciles will be adversely affected to the degree outlined above, many of them will be. These figures show only the direct costs: the costs which show up on a private customer's electricity bill. Presumably, most of the cost of renewable energy will be indirect, via increased prices in areas where production is energy-intensive (ICF International, 2012).

The zero-sum game

These measures might nevertheless be justifiable if they led to substantial and demonstrable environmental benefits. Initially, the main justification for subsidising renewable energy was the reduction in CO_2 emissions which would be achieved by changing the country's energy portfolio. But, as critics have pointed out right from the start, total CO_2 emissions of all participating industries *are already capped* at the European level, through the Emissions Trading Scheme (EU-ETS). Both the subsidisation of renewables and the ETS are potential instruments to cut carbon emissions – but they cannot be meaningfully combined. The use of renewable obligations simply dictates *how* the carbon reduction targets will be met.

ETS and RO/FiT represent completely different approaches to CO_2 reduction. ETS is a cap-and-trade scheme, whereby the government controls the total volume of emissions reduction, but remains, in theory, neutral with regard to *who* implements these reductions and *in what way*. The key assumption behind this approach is that it cannot be known in advance how a given volume of emission reductions can be achieved in the least costly way. It is this lack of knowledge which provides the case for a more open-ended process, which permits unexpected outcomes, rectification and incremental learning as people find the most efficient ways of reducing CO_2 output. When circumstances change and/ or new relevant facts are discovered, the new information will quickly be reflected in the price of emissions permits. This will, in turn, lead to adjustments in the abatement process, whereby relatively expensive abatement strategies are abandoned and relatively cheap ones extended.

In short, a cap-and-trade scheme attempts to replicate features

127

of the market discovery process, to the extent that this is possible within a politically imposed scheme. To the extent that an actual cap-and-trade scheme resembles the textbook model, it is similar to a carbon tax that does not discriminate between different sources of carbon. In practice, it does not work anything like the textbook model, because, even though permits are freely tradable once they have been allocated, the initial allocation itself is a heavily politicised process (see Sinclair, 2011). Presumably, only a source-neutral carbon tax can reduce the level of politicisation to a tolerable level. But cap-and-trade depoliticises at least aspects of carbon abatement.

In contrast, with RO/FiT and its accompanying schemes the government itself picks and dictates one particular course for achieving CO_2 reductions. Economically, this approach can be justified only when making the assumption that the government can identify a reduction strategy that will *eventually* be more cost-effective than its alternatives, but which private sector actors will nevertheless not choose. It is an application of the 'picking winners' philosophy of industrial policy. In this view, the building of successful industries is better left to governments than to markets because governments are perceived to have a more holistic and long-term perspective.

EU-ETS and RO/FiT are thus built on completely distinct philosophies. One can follow either one of these, but not both at the same time, or at least not one *within* the other. And yet this is exactly what operating the RO policy within ETS does. When the total number of CO_2 emissions is already capped through ETS, selectively reducing emissions in any one particular sector cannot decrease their overall level any further.[3] Subsidising renewables

---

3   As a theoretical extreme case, one could imagine a renewables subsidisation scheme on a scale so gigantic that it suffices to push overall emissions below

around since 1993 – these underwent a major extension from 2000 onwards under the umbrella of the Renewable Energies Act (EEG). In the German context, the marginal cost of abating CO_2 through the use of wind energy has been shown to be about €54 per tonne (Frondel et al., 2009: 13–14).[5] Meanwhile, the price of an emissions permit has never exceeded €30, and has fluctuated around €15 throughout most of 2010 and 2011 (EEX, 2012). For solar energy, the cost of abatement has been shown to be around €716 per tonne. In other words, an emitter of carbon is willing to pay, on the open market, around €15 for permission to produce another tonne of CO_2 and another emitter is willing to reduce their output by one tonne for precisely that level of compensation (whether through efficiency devices, producing a different mix of goods and services, and so on). On the other hand, to avoid producing another tonne of CO_2 through wind energy will cost well over three times as much. This means that the German economy as a whole could either have abated a much larger amount of carbon at the same cost, or it could have achieved the same amount of carbon abatement at a fraction of the cost.

Supporters of the EEG argue that the cost of renewable energy will fall as soon as the industry has taken off. But they have argued this since the industry's inception, and so far cost estimates have only increased (ibid.: 9–13). So, unsurprisingly, the rhetoric of the EEG's supporters has shifted over time, away from decarbonisation and towards other supposed benefits. The EEG has been presented as a job-creation engine, which, in a very narrow sense, it was. The sector now employs about 300,000 people. But each of

---

5   This is under the assumption that wind energy replaces a mix of gas-fired and coal-fired electricity generation. If the comparison was made vis-à-vis a mix that included nuclear energy, the cost of abatement would have to be much higher.

these jobs is heavily subsidised – in the photovoltaic industry, the average subsidy per job is €175,000 – with resources that have to be sucked out of other sectors of the economy, causing offsetting effects there. Consequently, empirical studies find at best short-term net job creation, owed to rigidities in the labour market which delay the offsetting effects. The more common finding is negative net employment effects (Frondel et al., 2009: 15–18; Sinclair, 2011: 188–95).

The important aspect of the German case study is that its outcomes are not specific to details of its implementation. The renewable energy sector in the UK has not yet reached the size of its German counterpart, but there is no reason why it should develop any more favourably. As far as costs are concerned, renewables in general are a very expensive way of generating energy, unless exceptional geographical conditions apply. While most conventional sources of energy production are similar in their cost per unit of output, onshore wind is about one and a half times as expensive, and offshore wind nearly twice as expensive (Sinclair, 2011: 87). *The Economist* therefore calls the promotion of offshore wind 'one of the costliest ways known to man of getting carbon out of the energy system'.[6] And yet, photovoltaic energy is twice as costly again (ibid.: 87).

Other outcomes are not specific to the German case study either. The fact that renewable energy subsidies in Germany have not led to overall emission reductions is simply due to the same ETS cap, which will also render any emission savings in the UK void – renewable subsidies will just lead to the price of CO_2 permits falling. And the reason why there has been no net

---

6   'Poles apart. Australia's plans for cutting carbon emissions are welcome, if imperfect. Britain's are fundamentally flawed', *The Economist*, 14 July 2011.

employment creation is that 'green jobs' are just another manifestation of the 'what is seen and what is not seen' fallacy explained long ago by Frédéric Bastiat.

What should be done?

A narrow response

There is neither a rational environmental nor an economic case for subsidising renewables. There would be no net increase in CO_2 emissions, nor a net job loss, if the promotion of renewable energy in the UK was scrapped in its entirety. Renewable energy promotion costs households in the bottom decile of the income distribution about 1 per cent of their total annual budget, so these households would benefit more than any other group from the fall in energy prices. To be sure, there is a flipside to the coin that CO_2 emissions are constant under the ETS scheme: if carbon abatement will no longer happen through renewables, it will have to happen in other ways, which will also involve costs. Given the enormous spread between the cost of carbon abatement through renewables and the price of emission permits, however, substantial net cost savings can be expected.

A broader response

Up until now, the goal of a drastic reduction in carbon emissions has been accepted as a given. Only the mechanism chosen to achieve it – or rather, the confusion of mechanisms – has been criticised, without questioning the goal itself. This section will go one step farther, even though it must be clarified right from the start that this area has become so vast and complex that only the very surface can be touched here.

It has been argued that the most cost-effective way of achieving the goal of reduced carbon emissions is to adopt a source-neutral carbon tax. A cap-and-trade scheme could be a tolerable substitute, but only if it is left to itself without any attempts to micro-manage carbon abatement.[7] There is nothing unconventional about this argument; it has long been a standard point made by economists in the climate change debate. Nevertheless, no government committed to combating climate change has thus far settled for a carbon tax or a cap-and-trade scheme, and then left it at that (see Sinclair, 2011, for an international overview of policy mixes). No government has confined itself to setting the level of carbon cuts, without trying to meddle further. All governments have followed activist, winner-picking approaches, trying to micro-manage and impose a preferred pattern of carbon reduction. In climate politics, the temptation for dirigisme, rent-seeking and pork-barrel spending appears to be just too great to resist, and it is doubtful that this could ever be otherwise.

Yet the case for mitigating climate change, rather than adapting to its consequences, has been based on idealised assumptions about the political decision-making process behind mitigation. The Stern review famously estimated the cost of climate change mitigation to be no more than 1 per cent of global GDP, while putting the cost of unmitigated climate change at between

---

7   In an ideal world, both policies would lead to the same outcome. A carbon tax would lead to a reduction in carbon emissions to their 'socially optimal' level, while in a cap-and-trade scheme, the carbon cap would itself be equal to the socially optimal level. To say the same thing backwards: the efficient carbon tax rate in a Pigouvian scheme should be equal to the price of a permit in a cap-and-trade scheme.

5 and 20 per cent (Stern, 2007). 'Cost', in this case, is not under-stood in a strictly monetary sense, but includes attempts to put a value on non-material consequences such as a loss in biodiversity. Following Stern, the case for mitigation appeared to be settled.

Unfortunately, such favourable cost–benefit ratios can be obtained only by assuming away the vagaries and biases of the political process. In these models, policymakers are assumed to always choose the most cost-effective options available. The polit-ical actors in this model would never be distracted by the pres-sures of business lobbyists or environmental activists pushing for wasteful measures that suit their own commercial or ideological agenda. They would never substitute prestige projects for sensible projects. If a measure turned out to be wasteful, it would immedi-ately be discarded and replaced as soon as the evidence became available because profane motives such as an unwillingness to admit past errors would never drive decision-making.

So far, real-world climate change politics could not have been farther away from this idealised notion, and it is legitimate to ask whether it can be realistically expected to ever move closer. Envir-onmentalist pressure groups frequently criticise the failure of current and previous mitigation policies to reduce CO_2 emissions and, in a literal sense, they are clearly right. Total CO_2 emissions in most developed economies are no lower than they were in the early 1970s and, where they have fallen, this has been a continua-tion of a longer-term downward trend (see Figure 6).[8] Certainly, in the UK, there has been no substantial fall in the last two decades.

8   Carbon *intensity*, in contrast, has clearly fallen in almost every developed econ-omy: much less CO_2 is emitted per unit of real GDP. But again, this is a continu-ation of a long-term trend. In the UK, CO_2 intensity has followed an almost linear downward trend for four decades (International Energy Agency, 2011), and thus since long before terms such as 'decarbonisation' were even known.

Figure 6   CO$_2$ emissions since 1971 (1971 = 100)

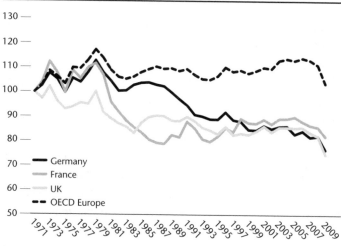

Source: Based on data from the International Energy Agency (2011)

Environmentalists typically conclude that mitigatory efforts are still 'not ambitious enough' and that 'more action is required'. This standard response completely ignores how far the mitigation approach has already been taken, and at what cost. If there is no visible impact on CO$_2$ levels, it is not for a lack of trying. It is because of the low cost-effectiveness of the measures chosen.

Of course, green taxes and regulatory measures could always be increased even further. But as long as the cost-effectiveness of these measures remains close to current levels, carbon mitigation can no longer be presented as a win-win option.

There is good reason to doubt whether CO$_2$ reduction policies could ever fundamentally improve, because the experience to date is too much in line with what public choice economics would predict. Carbon mitigation is, in essence, a multifaceted government mega-project. Myddelton (2007) explains the political economy of government *grands projets*, by reference to six prominent British case studies, and the dynamics he identifies are strikingly similar to the ones we observe in carbon mitigation. There is the same unrealistic optimism in the initial cost projections, which then make large cost overruns inevitable. Among its advocates, there is the same tendency to denigrate cost-effectiveness considerations as petty-minded, and the same unwillingness to consider the opportunity costs. There is the same tendency to escape into abstract rhetoric, rather than defending a project on the merits of tangible benefits.[9] There is the same unwillingness to abandon a project when it is evidently heading towards failure and to write off sunk costs. Among the electorate, there is the same lack of incentives to monitor a project's costs, or to mobilise discontent politically. No single voter has any impact on the project, nor is the cost to an individual taxpayer even readily identifiable.

Climate mitigation not only reflects but *exponentiates* the dynamics that Myddelton identifies. Unlike the *grands projets* Myddelton discusses, climate mitigation is not one single project with clear-cut boundaries and an identifiable timescale. It is a vast array of open-ended projects, a leitmotif that permeates many disparate areas of government activities. This makes it even harder for voters to monitor its performance critically. In short, if conventional government mega-projects are prone to breeding

---

9   Conventional government mega-projects have often been justified by appealing to a vague notion of 'national prestige' (Myddelton, 2007: 193–4). In climate mitigation, the 'exemplary function' is often emphasised, alongside 'responsibility for future generations'.

white elephants, climate mitigation must be prone to breeding them in herds.

So much for the costs; what about the benefits of mitigation? The Stern review, based on IPCC models, predicts global warming to cause damage equivalent to a loss of between 5 and 20 per cent of global GDP. These are drastic figures, but it is worth recalling their origin. The Stern report is a collection of six scenarios, with the 20 per cent figure pertaining to that which combines pessimistic assumptions about a number of unknowns. Interestingly, even Stern's ultra-pessimistic scenario does not predict major damage in the foreseeable future. It predicts the damage from global warming to remain almost flat until about the 2080s, and to rise slowly from then on, crossing the 10 per cent level in the second half of the 22nd century and reaching 13.8 per cent by 2200. It is only through the use of very low discount rates that damage predicted to occur in the very distant future is treated as if it were just around the corner. As Nordhaus (2007) explains:

> with near-zero discounting, the low damages in the next two centuries get overwhelmed by the long-term average over the many centuries that follow. In fact, using the [Stern] Review's methodology, more than half of the estimated damages 'now and forever' occur after the year 2800. [...] The large damages from global warming reflect large and speculative damages in the far-distant future magnified into a large current value by a near-zero time discount rate.

A number of problems arise when applying very low discount rates to long time periods. For example, using the same logic, one could also advocate large mandatory savings, in order for the generation living in 2800 to enjoy a higher capital stock. Climate mitigation, if it can be made to work, would amount to an intergenerational transfer from today's generations to distant-future generations. But the capacity to adapt to the consequences of climate change is a function of technology and the capital stock, which grow over time. The distant-future generations that will be affected will also be much more resilient and adaptive (see Dawson, 2008; Lawson, 2009: 34–8, 82–90; Sinclair, 2011: 21–6).

Nordhaus runs a simulation similar to Stern's, using a slightly higher discount rate, and reaches completely different conclusions. The social cost of carbon is now down to one tenth of Stern's estimate, which still provides a case for carbon reduction, but on a far more modest scale than proposed in the Stern review. Indeed, the Stern review is the outlier in the literature, and the deviation is mostly due to the difference in discount rates. Other models have consistently found a case for some limited action on climate mitigation, but not for drastic measures (Lomborg, 2007: 37–48, 190–97).

Unless we treat 'combating climate change' as a moral absolute, there is a strong case for rebalancing policies away from mitigation and towards adaptation. The latter have a much better chance of actually working. Adaptation almost always involves *local* responses to very specific local problems. Activities such as investing in flood protection or irrigation systems can be addressed at the regional and local levels. They can be much better monitored and evaluated by electorates, not only because they take place at a lower level and on a smaller scale, but also because their objectives are much narrower and more specific. Erecting flood protection is a more tangible objective than 'decarbonising the economy' or 'saving the planet'. Adaptation requires expansions of already existing programmes rather than the rolling out of entirely new ones. This is because global warming does not bring up fundamentally new challenges – it *aggravates* challenges that already exist and that need to be tackled anyway (Lawson, 2009: 39–46). Malaria prevention, for example, is sensible under any climate scenario.

Summary

Thus, how should we be framing the poverty debate in the context of the politics and economics of climate change? While a strong case has been made for being sceptical about expensive CO_2 abatement policies, it is accepted that some might see a case for intervention here. In this debate, however, those informing the political debate on poverty should point out the trade-offs involved. Secondly, even if the decarbonisation agenda is accepted, governments are pursuing that agenda in a way which is monumentally inefficient, thus raising energy costs, especially for the poorest. Certainly, the poverty lobby should be pointing this out. Policies such as aiding credit-constrained households with improvements in the energy efficiency of their homes, which help low earners to reduce their fuel bills while also incidentally reducing CO_2 emissions, are defensible. But we should be a lot warier about policies that lower the living standards of low earners in the name of climate mitigation more generally.

7 REGRESSIVE TAXATION

*As Colbert, the great 17th century reformer of the French tax system
is reputed to have said, the art of taxation is to pluck the goose
so as to obtain the largest amount of feathers, with the smallest
possible amount of hissing. It is on this basis that, for many
years, I and my predecessors and successors as Chancellor of the
Exchequer in this country (and many of our counterparts elsewhere
in Europe) have used high-sounding health arguments to justify
raising substantial revenues from tobacco taxation, always taking
care not to pitch the duty so high that too many people gave up
smoking, causing the tax yield actually to diminish.*

NIGEL LAWSON (2009)

Few elder statesmen have been as frank, even in retrospect, about
the use of 'sin taxes' as Nigel Lawson. But they have made copious
use of them, even though the low price elasticity of demand for the
goods upon which they are levied is well known (e.g. Townsend,
1996). Sin taxes do reduce 'sinning' to a degree, but they impose a
disproportionate burden on low earners.

The two most important types of sin taxes, alcohol and
tobacco duties, officially account for almost 5 per cent of the
disposable income of households in the bottom income quintile.
But this figure represents a huge understatement, because it is
derived from expenditure surveys, and thus based on self-reported

consumption patterns. It has long been established that expenditure on socially stigmatised products is under-reported in official surveys (e.g. Attanasio et al., 2006). This can be shown by comparing reported consumption with consumption recorded in the national accounts or, in other words, by comparing the quantities people report they buy with the quantities that are actually being bought and sold. Just under 50 per cent of all recorded alcohol sales, and just under 40 per cent of all recorded tobacco sales, show up in the expenditure surveys (Brewer and O'Dea, 2012). This type of under-reporting cannot be attributed to specific parts of the income distribution but, if it is at least vaguely proportional to actual consumption, then alcohol and tobacco duties could well cost low earners about a tenth of their income (see Table 22).

Table 22 **The cost of 'sin taxes' to households in the bottom quintile of the income distribution**

	Alcohol	Tobacco	Sum
Duties as % of disposable income of the bottom quintile (by equiv. income)	1.6%	3.2%	4.8%
Self-reported spending as % of recorded spending (according to national accounts)	<50%	<40%	n/a
Spending corrected for under-reporting (assuming under-reporting is independent of income)	3.2%	7.5%	10.7%

Sources: Based on data from ONS (2011b) and Brewer and O'Dea (2012)

In spite of the obvious implications, this is also a topic which the poverty campaigners prefer to avoid. CPAG (2005: 32) has even defended sin taxes in an awkward way:

Some taxes, though regressive, are designed to influence consumption behaviour rather than raise money – the so-called 'sin taxes' on tobacco and alcohol. Whereas policy makers might not wish to change such taxes, the overall balance [of the tax system] is significantly awry.

It is a topic over which paternalistic and egalitarian inclinations collide. Snowdon (2012a: 52) summarises this conflict:

Reformers are never likely to fret about 'beer poverty' in the same way as they worry about 'fuel poverty'. [...] Sin taxes are doubly regressive because they tend to target products which are disproportionately consumed by the poor. Those who campaign for the minimum pricing of alcohol – a sin tax by any other name – explicitly target drinks consumed by the poor and homeless while assuring the middle-class that their chardonnay will go untouched. The healthist agenda, enshrined on the Left in the rhetoric of 'health inequalities', is so dominant that it can overwhelm traditional concerns about poverty and inequality.

At this point, it is not necessary to get into the vexed debate about whether government should interfere with personal lifestyle choices at all, rather than treating them as a purely private matter. But the economic case is straightforward. If price elasticity of demand is low, sin taxes necessarily have to tear a large hole in the budgets of low earners before they can lead to a modest reduction in the respective habit. By implication, this also means that a decrease in sin taxes would not lead to a substantial increase in 'sinning', but would mostly free up money for other uses by the poor. Unless the price elasticity of demand is zero, however, and available estimates suggest that it is not, then a decrease in sin taxes would probably also lead to some increase in the consumption of the taxed good.

Ultimately, the question is one of whether we conceive the reduction of unhealthy habits in terms of a trade-off, or an absolute imperative which is worth any price. If we take the latter view, then details about the price elasticity of demand, offsetting effects, unintended consequences, etc., are unimportant. In this framework, the aim of decreasing the consumption of alcohol and tobacco overrides all other considerations. If we take the former view, a small increase in drinking or smoking might well be considered a price worth paying if it enables a noticeable increase in low earners' living standards.

Snowdon (ibid.: 42–51) summarises the literature on the price elasticities of demand for alcohol and tobacco. Both fall into a range between −0.3 and −0.5, such that a price increase of 10 per cent would reduce the quantity consumed by up to 5 per cent. Consumption of tobacco and alcohol is thus responsive to price, even if not very much so. But a number of problems come up when disaggregating these figures a bit. Firstly, elasticity figures vary by consumption intensity, with moderate/occasional consumers being the most price-sensitive. Thus, sin taxes target exactly the wrong subgroup, mostly deterring modest consumers. Secondly, at least in the case of tobacco, newer studies tend to find lower elasticity figures than older ones. Given the long-term decline in the prevalence of smoking, this is not at all surprising. Four decades ago, about one in two adults smoked; today, the rate is down to one in five (see Table 23). The 'marginal smoker', who is most easily deterred by a tax or a comparable measure, gave up smoking long ago. The smaller the population of smokers becomes, the less responsive to taxation it will be.

Table 23 **Cigarette smoking prevalence in the UK over time**

	Male	Female
1970	55%	44%
1980	42%	35%
1990	31%	29%
2000	29%	25%
2010	21%	20%

Source: ONS data, taken from Cancer Research UK (2012)

Sin taxes are an especially inefficient way of curbing unhealthy habits, and have become more so over time. Price elasticity is already relatively low even at an aggregate level, and lower still among the subgroups with high levels of consumption. If the government must get involved, it could directly help those who *want* to quit their habits, for example subsidising products and services that facilitate smoking cessation. But the aim of 'promoting healthy living' does not justify a steeply regressive form of taxation. When it comes to raising low earners' living standards, cutting sin taxes substantially should be seen as a low-hanging fruit.

For example, cutting alcohol and tobacco duty by half would be equivalent to increasing low earners' income by around 5 per cent, and this is without even looking at the taxes levied upon other 'sins' such as gambling. The government also collects almost £13 billion in alcohol and tobacco duties per year, however. Revenue losses arising from cutting these rates would partially have to be balanced through increasing other taxes and, while almost any realistic alternative would be less regressive than alcohol and tobacco duties, many are economically more distorting. The government should therefore try to achieve spending cuts in the same area. Snowdon (2012b) documents how various arms of government sponsor a vast industry of anti-smoking and (on a lesser scale) anti-drinking groups. Needless to say, these groups have every right to campaign for any lifestyle changes and/or changes in legislation they choose. But since the health risks associated with smoking and drinking are practically universally known, no public good argument can be made for subsidising their activities with tax money. They are simply private interest activities and, as such, they should be entirely privately funded.

8 WORK – SUPPLY AND DEMAND

Work is better than its reputation

One of the most often-repeated claims of the poverty campaign groups is that work is not a route out of poverty (see Oxfam, 2011: 4; Oxfam, 2010b; CPAG, 2010b, 2009a, 2009b, 2008). The terms 'work' and 'employment' are seldom used with positive connotations, but rather in conjunction with adjectives such as 'menial', 'insecure' or 'stressful'. This leads them to reject anti-poverty policies based on raising work levels. CPAG (2008: 5) bemoans 'an overreliance on paid work as the route out of poverty – which it certainly isn't for a substantial number of people'. Oxfam (2010b: 2) also attacks a perceived 'single-minded *focus on promoting paid employment as the only goal*' (emphasis in the original), because 'this narrow focus leads to a failure to recognise the extent of in-work poverty, which now exceeds out-of-work poverty' (ibid.).

The poverty campaigners are not saying that low earners should not work. They have written extensively about the need to 'create better jobs' and 'tackle complex structural barriers'. But these arguments remain on such an abstract level that it is difficult to recognise any policy implications from them. When it comes to tangible demands, the core message is that raising out-of-work benefits is much more important than raising work levels. The statistic most frequently quoted by the poverty campaign groups is the share of children in relative poverty who already have a parent in work: 'Despite the Government conviction that work is the best route out of poverty, half of all poor children live with a working parent' (CPAG, 2008: 11).

In work or out of work? In poverty or out of poverty?

The scepticism about paid work is mistaken. Work *is* a route out of poverty.

One of the basic errors of the poverty activists is that they effectively treat both work and poverty as binary variables, with people being either 'in work' or 'out of work' and/or either 'in poverty' or 'out of poverty'. Yet it is more accurate to treat labour market attachment as a continuum or, even better, as a coordinate system, with the number of hours worked per week on one axis, and the proportion of the year (or a longer period) spent in a job on the other axis. Otherwise, full-time employment is lumped together with minor employment, and steady employment with casual employment.

As far as the first 'axis' – weekly working hours – is concerned, even a slightly more nuanced look at the data provides a very different impression. Table 24 shows the rates of material deprivation (MD), a consumption-based poverty measure, among households with children, differentiated according to parental work status. Instead of the binary working/workless distinction used by the poverty activists, three different possible work statuses – full-time, part-time and workless – are considered, with different possible combinations in households with more than one adult. This is still a very high level of aggregation but it already shows a clear correlation between labour-market attachment and material deprivation.

Table 24 **Material deprivation and low income among households with children by parental employment status, 2009**

Family status and work status of parent(s)	Material deprivation rate
Single parent, not working	54%
Couple, both not working	54%
Couple, at least one in part-time work	35%
Single parent in part-time work	17%
Couple, one in full-time work, one not working	14%
Single parent in full-time work	7%
Couple, one in full-time work, one in part-time work	2%
Couple, both in full-time work	1%

Source: Gathered from ONS and DWP (2011: 88)

These data do *not* show that raising parental work levels would be sufficient to eradicate material deprivation poverty. Part of the data must be explained by a selection bias, with higher-skilled parents also being more likely to work longer hours and receive higher pay. What it does suggest, however, is that the in-work poor are rarely in full-time, year-round employment.

The alleged substitution of in-work poverty for out-of-work poverty, which the poverty activists denounce, is really a substitution of part-time employment and poverty for worklessness. Between 1996 and 2010, the number of children in households with no adult in paid work fell from 2.9 million to 2.1 million. Meanwhile, the number of children in households with one or two adults in part-time work, but none in full-time work, increased from 0.9 million to 1.4 million (ONS and DWP, 2012a: 120). This development has mostly been driven by previously workless single parents finding part-time work. While it is still the lowest in Europe, the employment rate of single parents has risen by more than 10 percentage points since the mid-1990s.

Although achieved at a very high fiscal cost, this was one component of the 1997 Labour government's anti-poverty strategy that could be called a qualified success. The main factor explaining this 'success' is working tax credit (WTC), and its predecessor, the working families' tax credit (WFTC) (Brewer et al., 2006; Brewer and Shephard, 2004). Working tax credit provides a substantial incentive to work for a certain number of hours a week. The downside is that it also discourages people from working for longer than that number. Working tax credit is conditional on a minimum number of hours worked, with a threshold of 16 hours for single parents, 24 (previously 16) for parental couples, and 30 hours for single adults. From then on, provided a minimum income threshold has been crossed, a taper rate of 41 per cent applies. If it combines with income tax and national insurance, it results in an effective marginal tax rate of 73 per cent. So, unsurprisingly, the typical working hours of single parents receiving working tax credit are clustered at the threshold. Of the 1.01 million single parents receiving working tax credit, 0.55 million work for 16 hours or a little more. Among parental couples receiving working tax credit, 0.23 million out of 0.92 million are clustered in this range of working hours (ONS and HMRC, 2012). Thus, the high levels of poverty are concentrated among those working a relatively small number of hours.

Considering the second 'axis' – the duration of employment periods – Browne and Paull (2010) show that work *retention* over time is more important for living standards than work status in a snapshot perspective. This is particularly relevant among single parents, who have lower work-retention rates than other groups.[1]

Work retention is positively associated with various measures of work progression, such as increases in hourly wages. The data do not permit strong conclusions, because the causation may well go the other way round (or both ways round): rather than wage increases being a reward for work retention, employees who expect that they will progress in work are more likely to stay than those who see no such prospects. Either way, it is difficult to imagine a situation in which work progression is more likely outside the labour market than inside.[2]

The report follows individuals over a period of three years, thereby not accounting for the longer-term effect of work retention. The two dimensions of labour-market attachment that are mentioned are weekly workload and work retention, and they are not independent of each other. Browne and Paull (2010: 32–51) show that weekly workloads tend to increase with the duration of employment, and that full-time employees are more likely to progress in work than part-time employees.

In short, once working hours and retention are accounted for, work is a much safer bet than the poverty campaigners believe. Looking just a little bit below the surface of the aggregates which the poverty campaigners cite leads to completely different policy conclusions. A comprehensive anti-poverty strategy ought to aim

---

1   'Retention', in this case, refers to the workforce as a whole, not any particular employer. Changing jobs frequently is still counted as work retention.

2   For a skilled worker who has recently lost their job, it is, of course, entirely sensible to take the time for a proper, thorough job search and preparation, instead of accepting the first available job offer. This is why a distinction between the functions of unemployment insurance and welfare is sensible. Strategies of raising work levels relate to welfare recipients, not those in retraining or short-term unemployment.

at raising the labour-market attachment of welfare recipients towards a work level approximating full-time, all-year employment. Part-time and/or short-term employment can be sensible first steps, but they should not be judged by impossible standards. Of course, a two-day-a-week job or a short-term employment spell will seldom raise somebody's annual income above 60 per cent of the national average. But this does not mean that such opportunities are no improvement over the alternative. We should remember too that the benefits systems as it stands provides no particular incentive for long-term labour-market attachment or for working the number of hours that would lead to a decisive movement out of poverty – the marginal tax and benefit withdrawal rates are just too high over a very long income spectrum.

It is worth noting that this section has been limited to the *pecuniary* gains from work and has not even discussed the relationship between work and indicators of mental health, social capital or children's educational attainment (see Kay, 2010).

Workless households: scale and significance

Child poverty has tended to dominate the poverty debate in recent years. Here, poverty campaigners especially underrate the importance of parental work. Their focus is, again, on a crude aggregate – the overall employment rate:

> High employment rates do not necessarily mean that child poverty is reduced. The UK employment rate has remained above 70 per cent for the past decade. However, if simply having a high employment rate was in itself the primary way to tackle child poverty, the UK would already have achieved lower levels of child poverty. (CPAG, 2008: 11)

But the aggregate employment rate is a meaningless figure in the context of child poverty. In the UK, the overall employment rate hides a highly polarised cross-household distribution of employment, with many dual-earner households, but also many 'zero-earner households' (see, for example, Simon and Whiting, 2007).[3] During the past decade, the share of children in households with no adult in paid employment has been steady at around 17 per cent, without much year-on-year fluctuation around this average (Eurostat, 2012). This is comfortably the highest rate in Europe (see Figure 7), even though it already represents a considerable improvement compared with the mid-1990s, when the rate was over 20 per cent. But, worryingly, progress stalled long ago in reducing the zero-participation rate for households with children. Almost all the improvement occurred during the second half of the 1990s.

From these figures alone, one would expect very high child poverty figures for the UK. But overall poverty figures are the combined result of 'incidence effects' and 'composition effects'. Figure 8 plots the share of children in workless households against the material deprivation poverty rate among those households. It shows that the UK comes out exceptionally well on the material deprivation rate – it is the second-lowest among the neighbouring countries, only slightly undercut by Sweden. In other words, material deprivation among workless households in the UK is low. This should lead one to question whether the absence of state income transfers is the cause of child poverty.

Child poverty campaigners essentially argue that policymakers

---

3   Another reason why the overall employment rate is irrelevant in terms of child poverty is that in the UK, employment rates are also relatively high among couple households *without* children (Eurostat, 2009: 48).

Figure 7   **Proportion of children in workless households, EU-27, average 2000–10**

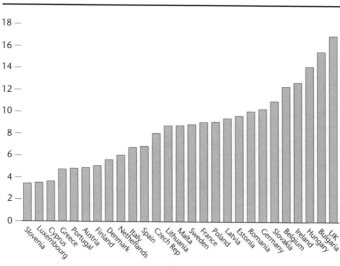

Source: Eurostat (2012)

should ignore the x-axis, and try to move further 'downwards' on the y-axis. This monograph, on the other hand, prioritises a move 'leftwards' along the x-axis.

One of the reasons for the high proportion of children in workless households is the high prevalence of single parenthood in the UK. For obvious reasons, employment rates among single parents are generally lower than among two-parent households (Eurostat, 2009: 48). But this is only part of the explanation. Figure 9 plots the prevalence of single parenthood in Europe against the employment rates among single parents. It shows two polar cases: countries where employment rates among single

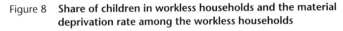

Figure 8 **Share of children in workless households and the material deprivation rate among the workless households**

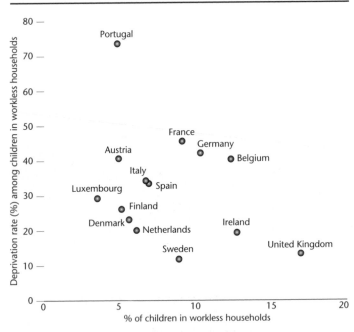

Sources: Based on data from Eurostat (2012) and UNICEF (2012)

parents are low but where this household type is not very common (for example, Belgium and Poland); and countries where single parenthood is very common but most of them work (for example, Sweden and Denmark). Most countries come out somewhere in between these cases. The outlier is the UK, with both the highest proportion of children in single-parent households and the lowest proportion of single parents in work.

About 11 per cent of children in the UK live with a workless

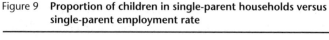

Figure 9   **Proportion of children in single-parent households versus single-parent employment rate**

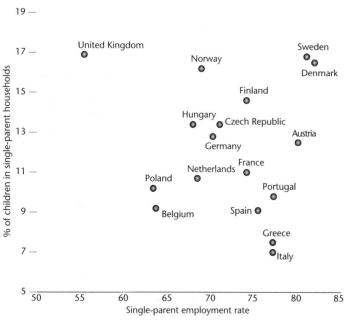

Sources: Based on data from Eurostat (2009) and UNICEF (2005)

single parent and another 6 per cent of children live with a single parent who works part-time (which mostly means a sixteen-hour working week for reasons discussed above). These figures represent a significant improvement. In the mid-1990s, the employment rate of British single parents was as low as 43 per cent. There has been progress up to a point, but it has not been built upon for a long time. Altogether, just under 28 per cent of all children in the UK live in a household with nobody in full-time employment

(ONS and DWP, 2011); and, as noted above, 17 per cent of children live in a household where no adults work either full-time or part-time (see Table 25). If this constitutes an 'over-reliance on paid work as the route out of poverty', what would count as an 'under-reliance'?

Table 25 **Percentage of British children in households with no adult in full-time employment**

	Single parent	Parental couple	Total
Workless	10.8	6.2	16.9
Part-time work	6.2	4.6	10.8
Total	16.9	10.8	27.7

Note: The cells in the table denote percentages as a percentage of the population as a whole. For example, 10.8 per cent of British children are in a workless single-parent household and just under 17 per cent are in a workless single-parent or couple household.
Source: Based on data from ONS and DWP (2011)

Single parenthood: a digression

Hardly any other country in the world spends so much on family benefits as the UK. All the Nordic and continental social democracies, except France, have been overtaken on this count. And yet, to many recipients, it does not feel that way. Furthermore, claims that spending is still far too low have never abated. The main reason for the disconnect between high spending and mediocre outcomes is to be found in the underlying risk profiles. With a very high proportion of children living in single-parent households, and a very low proportion of single parents in paid work, the UK has a demographic profile that is prone to producing high levels of child poverty. For the poverty activists, single parenthood is a taboo topic. For them, discussing single parenthood means 'blaming the victim' and 'demonising the poor'. And yet, child poverty rates cannot be meaningfully compared across countries without accounting for differences in the demographic risk factors that help explain poverty.

Unfortunately for economists, debates about single parenthood in the political sphere almost always degenerate into a debate about 'family values', and about how to evaluate the social changes that have taken place since the 1960s. In this debate, both the 'socially conservative' and the 'socially liberal' are missing one major point. The important fact is not that there are more single parents now than there were in the 1950s. That is obvious and unsurprising. The interesting questions, which are so far unresolved, should be:

- Why does the prevalence of single parenthood vary so much across countries that have, in one way or another, experienced the same social changes since the 1960s? The social stigma and economic hardship that were once associated with single parenthood have disappeared in the UK – but they have also disappeared in Belgium, the Netherlands and France, where one in ten children, rather than one in five, live with a single parent.
- Why does the skill profile and age profile of single parents differ across countries which have, again, experienced very similar changes in social values? Single parenthood is not always and everywhere a poverty risk. It depends on the level of education and work experience at the time of becoming a single parent.

The latter point refers to the composition of the single-parent population, which is much more important than the number of single parents. Blundell (2001) compares the profiles of single parents in the UK and Germany and two differences stand out: in the UK, single parenthood is much more heavily concentrated among the unskilled than in Germany; and British single parents tend to have children at a younger age. In Britain, 69 per cent of single parents have no formal qualification beyond compulsory schooling, compared with 35 per cent of their German counterparts. The average age among British single mothers whose youngest child is below the age of four is twenty-eight, compared with thirty-two in Germany (ibid.: 105–7). Four years may not seem like a large difference, but given that such mothers fall into an age range which is of particular relevance in acquiring work experience, the implications need no spelling out. This is particularly true in the case of teenage births, where the UK also records the highest rate in western Europe (UNICEF, 2005: 31).

The above two points have deliberately been formulated as questions – no attempts will be made here to provide an answer, which would have to spread well beyond the boundaries of this monograph if not beyond the boundaries of economics more generally. All that can be done here is to formulate a very general 'no-regrets' policy which would be sensible regardless of the answers to the above questions.

Even if it turned out that the tax and benefit system was only a minor factor in explaining the particular pattern of single parenthood in the UK, it would still be sensible not to penalise the formation of joint households. Two features of the tax and benefit system are especially problematic in this regard. The first is the fact that the tax system and the benefit system deal with different units of account: tax liability is assessed at the individual level, while benefit entitlement is assessed at the household level. This results in a 'couple penalty': if a non-working single parent lives with a working partner (whether they marry or not), the working partner's earnings will be counted against the non-working partner's benefit entitlement. The tax liability of the working partner, however, will not be diminished. The couple penalty is a feature of both the current system and the coming 'universal credit'.

This problem could be removed by introducing a tax-free allowance for every household member, which would be freely transferable within the household. With an allowance of £X for the first adult, £Y for the second adult and £Z for every child, a parental couple with two children would attain a joint tax-free allowance of £(X+Y+Z+Z). The system would be neutral with regard to how partners split working hours between them.

There is nothing new about this idea. The earnings disregard for the universal credit will be set in a similar way (see DWP, 2011), and until the late 1970s, the same was true for tax-free allowances for married couples both with and without children. The abolition of this system of tax allowances was a classic case of 'throwing out the baby with the bathwater'. Critics noted that since this was a system of tax relief rather than cash benefits, it did not help those whose earnings were below the tax-free allowance. They were right – but this was a feature that could have been changed within the system. It resulted from the separation of the tax system and the benefit system. In an integrated model such as a Friedmanite negative income tax, a household's benefit entitlement would depend on the distance between a household's income and their tax-free allowance (see Niemietz, 2011: 204–6).

REDEFINING THE POVERTY DEBATE

A second feature of the current system which constitutes a bias against the formation of joint households is the fact that several benefits contain a per-household element. If a household splits into two, this element can be received twice and if the households are merged, one of the payments is cancelled.[4] Of course, running a one-person household does not cost half as much as running a two-person household. The benefits system, relatively speaking, however, overcompensates one-adult households compared with two-adult households.

Table 26 shows what this can mean in practice. The first column shows the situation of a single parent with one young child, who qualifies for the standard rates of the income transfers. The second column shows the situation of a two-parent family with two children qualifying for the same transfers. In equivalised terms (i.e. after allowing for the different living costs of a one-adult and a two-adult household), the latter household's income transfer from the state is about a quarter below that of the former. The two families also qualify for the same housing benefit rate. The bottom line of Table 26 shows that the benefits system overcompensates for the increased fixed costs that result from the splitting of a household into two separate ones. The benefit system does more than just ensure the two ex-partners are no worse off after splitting; it actually renders them financially better off.

---

4   This is true for working tax credit, for the family element of the child tax credit, and for housing benefit. A single parent with one young child, eligible for the standard rates of the above, will receive £4,415 per annum plus the rent of a two-bedroom flat in the lower third of the rental price range. If this single parent now moves in with another single parent in precisely the same situation, the new joint household will also receive £4,415 p.a. plus the rent of a two-bedroom flat.

Table 26 **The 'couple penalty' illustrated**

	Single parent, one young child, works 16 hours per week	Couple, two young children, work 16 hours per week each
Working tax credit, basic element	£1,920	£1,920
Working tax credit, couple element	–	£1,950
Working tax credit, Single-parent element	£1,950	–
Child tax credit, child element	£2,690	£5,380
Child tax credit, family element	£545	£545
Child benefit	£1,056	£1,750
Housing benefit	2-bedroom flat	2-bedroom flat
Sum	£8,160	£11,545
% of equivalised income needs assuming benefits for one-person household = 100% of living costs	100%	76%

The overall impact of any reform in this area may be small, and there would be no short-term effects at all. But it is low-hanging fruit. Making the benefit system neutral with regard to household composition, so that it neither favours nor disadvantages any household type, is also defensible on grounds of horizontal equity. A way to achieve this is to set the above-mentioned household allowances in such a way that, in equivalised terms, they are roughly equal across all household types. Changes in family status would then no longer lead to changes in benefit entitlement, in equivalised terms.

The argument here is not that the government should try to *promote* the formation of couple households or discourage single parenthood among the low-skilled. Rather, the government should remove the discrimination against couple households.

Single parenthood is not per se a poverty risk; it becomes one when it acts as a deterrent to building up skills and work experience. The relevant comparators here are Sweden and Denmark, where single parenthood is just as common as in the UK, but where the work level among single parents is exceptionally high. About eight out of ten Swedish and Danish single parents are in employment and, among them, three out of four work full-time (NOSOSCO, 2004: 14–15).[5] There are also other countries in Europe where employment rates among single-parent households are slightly *higher* than among couple households (Eurostat, 2009: 48).

Whether one agrees with the above or not, the demographic risk profile should at least form part of the poverty debate. Impulses for a rational debate about risk profiles cannot be expected to come from the current poverty campaign groups. They have simply overstretched the 'taboo zone': single parenthood must not be discussed, because that would mean 'blaming the victim'. But employment must not be discussed either, because that would also mean 'blaming the victim'. This is surely motivated by the best of intentions – protecting a group perceived as powerless from criticism – but it has also led to an anaemic poverty debate.

---

5   No doubt this has a lot to do with subsidised childcare in these countries, but as shown in Chapter 4, childcare is also highly subsidised in the UK.

Labour demand

Employment is, despite all claims to the contrary, an important route out of poverty. This section provides some discussion of how employment rates among low earners could be raised.

Employment protection legislation

The UK labour market has undergone major changes over the past few decades. In the far-reaching reforms of the 1980s and early 1990s, the legal privileges of trade unions were removed and Wage Councils were abolished. As a result, the British labour market became one of the freest in the world by modern standards. But while subsequent governments have shown no inclination to reverse the Thatcher/Major reforms, a different form of labour market intervention has become considerably more stringent since the late 1990s: employment protection legislation (EPL). In terms of employment protection legislation, the UK now occupies a middle-of-the-road position between the lightly regulated North American labour markets, and the tightly regulated ones of the major continental European economies. This is shown in the summary indicator by Gwartney et al. (2011), and confirmed by the Heritage Foundation's (2011) alternative indicator.

In the empirical literature, it is fairly well established that employment protection legislation has negative effects on employment among disadvantaged groups (for an overview, see Skedinger, 2010: 75–122). This does not mean that economists generally disapprove of employment protection legislation. Supporters argue that stronger employment protection legislation leads to a longer average duration of employment relationships, which encourages a more long-term approach to labour relations

– for example, increasing employers' willingness to invest in staff qualifications. But there is little doubt that, from the perspective of outsiders (those with a weak labour-market attachment or entirely outside it), employment protection legislation constitutes an entry barrier. This is shown in Table 27.

Table 27 **Employment protection legislation and unemployment**

	Index of hiring and firing regulations, 1995 Scale: 0–10 (10 = least intrusive)	Index of hiring and firing regulations, 2009	Unemployment rate, average 1995–2010	Long-term (>1 year) unemployment rate, average 1995–2010
Denmark	8.1	8.0	5.1%	1.1%
Switzerland	7.7	7.9	n/a	n/a
USA	7.1	7.1	5.6%	0.5%
Canada	6.5	6.3	n/a	n/a
UK	7.4	5.4	6.1%	1.7%
France	4.2	3.2	9.6%	3.7%
Italy	2.6	3.1	9.0%	5.1%
Germany	3.9	2.9	8.7%	4.4%
Spain	2.6	2.4	13.1%	5.0%

Sources: Gathered from Gwartney et al. (2011), Eurostat (2012)

British labour market outcomes during the interlude of relatively light-touch regulation have been largely positive – indeed, they have been among the best in the developed world, albeit never among the *very* best. Between 1993 and 2001, unemployment fell in every single year, and then averaged 5 per cent until the onset of the present recession. More importantly, around three-quarters of those unemployed at any given point in time were short-term unemployed, who would re-enter the labour market within a year. This stands in stark contrast to the major continental economies, where a substantial proportion of the unemployed remain so for a long time.

There are legitimate concerns about whether these relatively positive unemployment figures have revealed the full story in recent years. There was rapid job creation, but not all of these jobs were well paid and stable. Also, recipients of incapacity-related benefits – dubbed 'Britain's hidden reserve of long-term unemployed' by Carswell and Hannan (2008: 113) – never appeared in these statistics. There is only so much labour market institutions can achieve, however: they cannot by themselves overcome skills deficits or dysfunctional welfare institutions. Yet the fact that low unemployment rates have been recorded in a context of high overall employment rates shows that the labour market has been functioning reasonably well.

Employment protection legislation measures, not unlike increases in social spending, are easy to introduce in economically good times, but much more difficult to reverse again in economically leaner times. Already in 2005, Shackleton (2005: 33) was warning: 'So far, changes in employment protection in a generally buoyant UK labour market have not produced problems, but the position may look different should the economy face a downturn.'

This is precisely what has happened since 2008. Given the severity of the downturn and the bleak economic outlook since then, it is unlikely that any set of labour-market institutions could have prevented a surge in unemployment. But the important question is whether the current set-up of the labour market will permit a return to pre-recession employment levels once the economy recovers.

Employment tribunals

'Labour market regulation' is an abstract term. The level of activity at employment tribunals can be used as a barometer of the impact of labour market regulation on the ground. During the first half of the 2000s, employment tribunals recorded around 120,000 accepted claims per annum. Since then, the number has nearly doubled to about 220,000 (HM Courts and Tribunals Service and Ministry of Justice, 2011a: 4–5). But what is more revealing is the composition of claims. About a third of all claims can be classified as unrelated to the intensity of labour market regulation. These are the cases where employers have been accused of breaking the employment contract, of failing to pay the agreed wage in full, or failing to inform their employees about changes concerning them. In short, these are simply cases where employers fail to adhere to a contract to which they have voluntarily agreed. Dealing with such cases is arguably the proper role of the employment tribunal system (ETS).

But this still leaves more than two-thirds of cases which are directly regulation-induced. These cases are not about breaches of a voluntarily agreed contract, but about breaches of regulations that limit freedom of contract. About half of them concern offences which, until relatively recently, would not have constituted offences at all. The number of discrimination-related claims, for example, has risen sharply in both absolute and relative terms. They have now become more important than claims related to dismissals and redundancies, even though the latter have also increased in absolute terms (see Table 28). Another 30 per cent of claims concern regulations which attempt to shape details of the working contract, such as working time and wages. These variables would previously have been considered the remit of the contracting partners or their representatives such as trade unions. Cases have also increased in complexity, with more than half of them now involving lawyers.

Table 28 **Composition of claims brought to employment tribunals**

	1997	2010
Working Time Directive, part-time workers regulations, minimum wage	n/a	30%
Breach of contract, failure to inform/consult, etc.	29%	30%
Discrimination	9%	20%
Dismissal/redundancy pay regulations	54%	17%
Other	8%	3%
Total	100%	100%

Sources: Based on data from HM Courts and Tribunals Service and Ministry of Justice (2011a) and Shackleton (2002)

Employment tribunal system activities are not just a neutral barometer of the degree of labour market interference. The risk of litigation has itself become part of the cost of recruiting, by making it an increasingly risky activity to employ people. The median level of compensation payments is not excessive and the chance of success is not especially high. In the case of discrimination claims, between 50 per cent (for disability discrimination) and 70 per cent (for sex discrimination) of all claims are rejected by the tribunal, settled informally or withdrawn before the trial even really begins. When a case is won, median compensation awarded is typically in the range between £6,000 and £7,000. The problem with tribunal activities outside of the system's traditional remit is that they create a high level of uncertainty. Compensation awards are often unpredictable. Especially in discrimination-related cases, it is difficult to see how this could be otherwise. Establishing whether or not a discrimination offence has been committed can never be as clear-cut as establishing whether or not an agreed salary has been paid out. The latter cases are about an action, the former about a presumed underlying motive for an action. A higher degree of discretion and subjectivity is thus inevitable.

A glimpse of the uncertainty that this creates can be gathered from Table 29, which shows some distributional parameters of compensation payments. It shows that a substantial proportion of awards deviate significantly from median.

Table 29 **The distribution of awards from successful employment tribunal cases**

	Median award	% of awards >£10,000	% of awards >£20,000
Unfair dismissal	£4,591	28%	11%
Race discrimination	£6,277	41%	22%
Sex discrimination	£6,078	30%	13%
Disability discrimination	£6,142	34%	14%
Age discrimination	£12,697	59%	39%

Source: Based on data from HM Courts and Tribunals Service and Ministry of Justice (2011a)

The profile of a typical discrimination claim is not one of a poor individual at the margins of the labour market – though such people may suffer most from the reduced level of job creation. Compared with breach-of-contract claimants, discrimination claimants are more likely to be highly educated, better paid, to work for the public or the charitable sector, to work for a very large organisation, and to be covered by a trade union or staff association, while being much less likely to work in sectors such as manufacturing, construction, retail or the catering industry – see Table 30.

Table 30 **Profile of employment tribunal applicants, traditional and extended functions**

	Breach of contract	Discrimination
Claimant has higher education qualification	33%	43%
Median annual pay	£20,000	£21,600
Claimant works in public sector	11%	36%
Claimant works for non-profit/voluntary sector	6%	12%
Claimant works in manufacturing, construction, wholesale/retail, hotels/ restaurants	43%	29%
Claimant works for organisation with >250 employees	34%	60%
Employer runs a human resources or personnel department	54%	75%
Claimant is member of trade union or staff association	13%	46%
Trade union or staff association present at workplace	20%	52%
Claimant could join trade union or staff association	89%	98%

Source: Based on data from BIS (2010)

Those who use the new employment tribunal remits most frequently are also those most likely to have alternative means of resolution or protection available. They are concentrated in large organisations, which generally have formalised

non-discrimination policies and standardised internal procedures to deal with grievances. The employees who are most disadvantaged on conventional measures are not the typical users
of employment tribunals. But even though they are not using
it frequently, they are nevertheless paying their share of the
system's cost. For example, the risk of litigation can be a deterrent to hiring members of a protected group, in which case the
'protection' would really be a disservice. The empirical evidence
on this issue is not very strong, and does not yet permit definite
conclusions (Bell and Heitmueller, 2009; Jones and Jones, 2008;
Neumark and Stock, 2007; Acemoglu and Angrist, 2001). But it
is entirely possible that anti-discrimination legislation is reducing
the employment prospects of protected groups.

Interference with contractual freedom damages the position
of those with weak bargaining power in the labour market in
other ways. It is well established that employment-related regulation has a much greater impact on small companies than on
large ones (for an overview, see Urwin, 2011: 53–67). Also, the
regulatory cost imposed on companies through employment-
related regulation has fixed-cost elements. If a company with 500
employees hires a 501st employee, the 'marginal regulatory cost'
will be very low. It is greatest when an owner-managed company
hires its first employee. This has implications for anti-poverty
policy as much as for general economic policy. As Urwin (ibid.:
84–101) shows, small companies are much more likely to employ
people with characteristics which generally constitute disadvantages in the labour market. This is true whether somebody's disadvantage consists of a lack of formal skills, self-reported language
difficulties, a recent spell of economic inactivity, or simply being
a new entrant into the labour force. There is a direct relationship

between these variables and company size, which is best illus-trated by comparing both ends of the scale: companies with either fewer than twenty-five or more than five hundred staff members, which, together, employ just over a third of the workforce. This is shown in Table 31.

Table 31 **Proportion of disadvantaged employees by company size**

	Company size (No. of employees)	
Nature of disadvantage	<25	>500
No formal qualifications	10.2%	3.8%
Language difficulties	16.0%	8.0%
Economically inactive a year before	4.0%	1.7%
Aged 16–24	18.7%	8.8%

Source: Based on data from Urwin (2011: 87–93)

The author argues that this is because large companies need to rely on more formalised, standardised working procedures, including in recruitment. Thus, they rely on visible skill signals which are easy to measure and communicate. While this enables them to screen a larger pool of applicants, it also means that some of the more subtle, tacit skill signals may not be detected. Large companies will therefore generally favour applicants with more conventional occupational biographies.

In short, disadvantaged employees benefit from a flourishing sector of small and medium-sized enterprises. While it is conven-tional political rhetoric to pay lip-service to the importance of small companies, policymakers continue to enact costly and cumbersome regulations which burden this sector dispropor-tionately. It is not just employment protection legislation which constrains the growth of small businesses. In summary indicators on the ease of doing business, the UK scores highly on variables associated with *starting* a business, but much less so on variables associated with *expanding* it: see Table 32.

Table 32 **Business regulation, summary indicators, 10 = least restrictive**

Regulatory category	Score
Starting a business	9.6
Licensing restrictions	9.2
Extra payments/bribes/favouritism	8.1
Administrative requirements	3.4
Bureaucracy costs	2.0

Source: Gathered from Gwartney et al. (2011)

The UK does exhibit a high level of owner-managed businesses that do not expand and take on employees as might be expected. Given the characteristics of their employees, it could be argued that this inhibits efforts at poverty alleviation.

Implications for policy

Both in terms of the design of the benefits system and also the problems caused by labour market regulation, there are serious inhibitions to work in the UK. These difficulties are particularly acute for single parents, the less well off and those at the margins of the labour market. The government should end the penalties on family formation within the tax and benefits system. Furthermore, there would be many benefits from reducing labour market regulation.

Reducing regulation would seem to be knocking on open doors given the continual outcry against red tape. Public choice theory (e.g. Niskanen, 1968; Blankart, 2008: 153–4) suggests, however, that senior bureaucrats are at least partially self-interested and enhance their own careers by seeking an expansion of their bureau's size, scope and budget. Information asymmetries within the state apparatus, as well as a lack of incentives among policymakers to constrain the growth of the bureaucracy, will generally work in the bureaucrats' favour. For these reasons regulation is difficult to remove in practice. It is beyond the scope of this paper to address the policy implications of the public choice approach and how they relate to British conditions. Suffice it to say that in order to constrain regulatory growth, it is beneficial to interpret it as an economic phenomenon, rather than the expression of a risk-averse 'mandarin' mentality. To return to a recurring theme of this monograph, however – the poverty lobby is entirely silent on this issue.

9 WELFARE

The welfare system is riddled with poverty traps. There are three broad, interlocked problem areas which any serious attempt at welfare reform will need to address:

- Work incentives are highly polarised, and weakest for the weakest groups. This is true for incentives both to enter the labour market, and to advance within it.
- The welfare system fosters resentment and negative attitudes towards recipients.
- There are no effective tools to deal with those long-term recipients who have become so detached from the labour market that they no longer respond to financial incentives alone.

The current system's complexity could well be counted as a fourth problem, but this situation will be significantly improved through the introduction of the universal credit (UC), which is why it will be ignored here. This chapter will deal only with those features of the welfare system which will still be present when the transition to universal credit has been fully completed. It will address each of the above problem areas in turn, while also showing the relationships between them.

Polarised work incentives, polarised employment patterns

Employment patterns in the UK are highly polarised across households, especially those with children. As has been noted, 17 per cent of all children live in a household with no adult in work, while at least 38 per cent live in a dual-earner household (ONS & DWP, 2011: 82).[1] Most of the former live with a single parent, but worklessness is common enough among couple households, too.[2] The polarisation of employment patterns is mirrored by a polarisation of work incentives. This does not prove that the latter has caused the former, and labour market decisions are not exclusively determined by pecuniary incentives. And yet, regardless of whether the polarised incentive pattern has caused the polarised work pattern or not, it certainly does not help in overcoming it.

Summary measures of work incentives typically distinguish between the incentive to enter the labour market at all, and the incentive to increase earnings once in it. The former is typically measured by the 'replacement rate': the ratio of disposable income without work to disposable income that could be earned in a realistically attainable job. What is 'realistically attainable' depends on personal characteristics, especially skills, and needs to be modelled. The incentive to increase working hours is measured by the implicit or effective marginal tax rate (EMTR), which is the

---

1   'At least', because for households where the head is self-employed, the work status of the partner is not listed separately. Twelve per cent of all children live in self-employed households, and surely *some* of them must be dual-earner households.

2   Even if the share of children in single-parent families were to fall to the lowest level in Europe (which is 7 per cent, in Italy), and if relative rates of worklessness remained the same, the share of children in workless households would still be as high as one in ten.

share of increases in gross earnings which does not translate into an increase in disposable income. For the UK, estimates of the distribution of these variables across the population as a whole and specific subgroups are available from Adam and Browne (2010), Adam et al. (2006), Brewer and Browne (2006), Brewer et al. (2006), as well as Brewer and Shephard (2004).

The short summary is that work incentives are weakest for single parents and workless couples. For these groups, median replacement rates are around 70 per cent and effective marginal tax rates are just above this level. This will not change significantly when the transition to universal credit has been completed, because universal credit has been designed in such a way that no recipient is substantially better or worse off than in the present system.

Work incentives for single parents

The case of single parents is straightforward. Single parenthood is concentrated among the low-skilled (Blundell, 2001: 106), which limits the amount of earnings they could achieve in the labour market, at least in the short term and based on their observable characteristics. If they have no earned income or savings, single parents will more or less automatically qualify for the full rate of universal credit and child benefit. This combination of a relatively low denominator and a relatively high numerator will create a high replacement rate, leading to a weak incentive to enter the labour market.

The incentive will be strongest for entering work at a small number of hours per week, so that earnings remain below the income disregard. As soon as earnings exceed the disregard, the effective marginal tax rate jumps to 65 per cent, and as soon as they exceed the personal allowance, it jumps to 76 per cent. For the small minority of single parents whose earnings are so high that they will no longer qualify for universal credit, the effective marginal tax rate will be 32 per cent. For such people, there is no strong pecuniary reason for *not* using an opportunity to increase earnings further. But universal credit will cover a large part of the earnings range, and most single parents' earnings potential is limited. At the moment, only 13 per cent of all single parents are in the upper two quintiles of the income distribution. It is safe to say that 76 per cent will be the typical effective marginal tax rate for working single parents.

Work incentives for parental couples

The situation of couples is more difficult to generalise. This group is much more heterogeneous in terms of labour market characteristics and, if one partner's work status changes, work incentives change for the other partner. But for workless couples with children, the situation is generally similar to that of workless single parents. They will also qualify for the full rate of universal credit and child benefit, albeit requirements to look for work will be somewhat more stringent. If both are low-skilled and lack work experience, their earnings potential will also be limited, leading to high replacement rates and thus weak incentives to enter the labour market. Incentives will, again, be strongest to work for a small number of hours per week, so that the full rate of universal credit can be retained. As earnings exceed the disregard, the effective marginal tax rate also jumps to 65 per cent and then quickly to 76 per cent, where it remains for a wide range of income.

But once one partner's earnings are high enough for universal credit to be fully tapered away, the effective marginal tax rate for the other partner falls to 32 per cent (or zero below the basic rate tax threshold, which is now close to £10,000). This explains the polarisation: there is a substantial loss of benefits for a workless household once *one* partner enters work. But as soon as one partner achieves a sufficiently high level of earnings, there are no strong disincentives that would stop the second partner from entering the labour market as well.

The general distribution of work incentives

For those who are already well established in the labour market and out of the benefits trap there are no strong disincentives against advancing further. But for those who are not yet well established, there is little incentive to get started, or to move beyond minor employment. The combination of universal credit withdrawal, income tax and national insurance makes the system look like a ladder on which the lowest rungs are farthest apart.

This is shown in Figure 10. The figure does not contain precise income ranges because they depend too much on variables which can differ a lot, especially the housing cost element of universal credit (the current housing benefit) and the number of children.

It should be noted that there are some additional quirks not shown in the figure. For example, once the earnings of the highest earner in a household reach £50,000, child benefit will be withdrawn. When this happens, the effective marginal tax rate can rise significantly.

The 50 per cent additional rate of income tax for top earners has been abolished precisely because it damages work incentives.

Figure 10 **Effective marginal tax rates by household income under the universal credit**

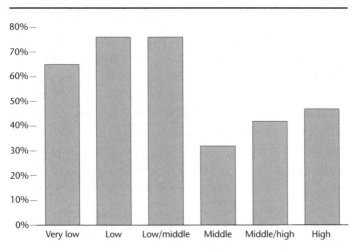

Yet, ironically, in the lower range of the income distribution, a far higher effective marginal tax rate of 76 per cent will remain the typical rate.

Does this matter?

In the worldview of the poverty campaigners, work incentives lead a strange double life. On the one hand, poverty campaigners deny the possibility that high benefits could undermine recipients' willingness to enter the labour market. But, at the same time, the fact that these benefits are tapered away at relatively steep rates as people increase their earnings is presented as a disincentive. The poverty campaigners are effectively saying that benefits themselves do not deter anybody from working, but their withdrawal suddenly does.

For example, CPAG (2008: 25) argues: 'low benefit rates demoralise those out of work and generate health problems that drive them away from employment, not closer to it'. Or more succinctly: 'current benefits are so low they undermine capacity and morale to engage with the labour market' (ibid.: 11). Raising out-of-work benefit rates is thus presented as a win-win option, which decreases poverty and simultaneously raises work levels. Veit-Wilson (2007: 2) asserts: 'The idea that people choose between employment or welfare benefits on the basis of narrow calculations is simply an economic theory which is not supported by evidence from the real world.'

Astonishingly, however, as soon as taper rates apply, the arguments change: 'Means-tested benefits worsen the poverty trap because they are withdrawn as earnings rise' (CPAG, 2009b: 27).

It is more expedient to be consistent and follow the standard approach in labour market economics, which is to treat work search effort as a continuum, not an either-or. Work search effort can be approximated by, for example, the weekly number of hours people spend job hunting, or the reservation wage. Such variables can take on an almost infinite number of values: they are almost never a yes-or-no decision. In such models, replacement rates or a close equivalent almost always come out as a significant determinant of work search effort, despite substantial disagreement about the importance of replacement rates relative to other factors (Blundell, 2001; Meghir and Phillips, 2008; Krueger and Mueller, 2008a; Krueger and Mueller, 2008b; Layard et al., 2005; Meyer, 1990; Feldstein and Poterba, 1984). Incentives matter. We may not know how much exactly they matter, but that they matter we know.

What should be done?

Improving work incentives does not necessarily mean cutting benefits. Transfer payments differ on many more dimensions than just their level, and much of their effect depends on the conditions under which they are granted. In the current British system, this can be seen by comparing four different instruments: income support, child tax credit, the basic rate of working tax credit and the 30-hour element of working tax credit.

Child tax credit and working tax credit are fairly generous, given that they come on top of child benefit, and that many other countries do not even have an equivalent. Income support and the 30-hour elements are rather basic payments. Yet when their impact is evaluated in a labour market model, the level of these payments is not the most important aspect. The main difference is in the access criteria. Child tax credit and income support are not work-contingent. Recipients are not required to work, to seek work, to prepare for work, or to engage in a work-related activity. Working tax credit is very different in that people can qualify only if they spend a specified minimum number of hours in paid employment. As the name implies, the same applies to the additional 30-hours element which is an extra working tax credit tranche activated once a recipient works for 30 hours.

These complexities are illustrated in Table 33. In theory, the means-tested version of jobseekers' allowance could also have been included in the bottom right cell, because it requires recipients actively to seek work and to be available for job offers. But since conditionality for jobseekers' allowance is not generally monitored and enforced, it is a less clear-cut case.

Table 33 **Conditionality versus generosity**

	Unconditional	*Conditional*
Generous	Child tax credit	Basic rate of working tax credit
Basic	Income support	30-hour addition to working tax credit

Shifting payments 'rightwards' towards conditionality is an alternative policy to moving them 'downwards' in an effort to save money. Conditional welfare ought to have an in-built, self-limiting tendency, by making the receipt of a transfer conditional on conduct that reduces the need for the transfer.

The principle of conditionality is easiest to apply in the case of in-work benefits. The theoretical case for in-work benefits is that they top up low earnings both in absolute terms and also relative to out-of-work benefits. They were presented as the way to raise the living standards of low earners while strengthening, rather than eroding, work incentives. Working tax credit really has mobilised some people into work. But it seems to have exhausted its potential. There was also an assumption that, once people were in work, they would eventually move on to a workload closer to full-time work. This has not materialised. Indeed, 41 per cent of all working tax credit recipients – 26 per cent among couples and 55 per cent among single parents – work for sixteen hours a week or just above. Why does working tax credit not mobilise more people, and why does it not encourage those it has mobilised to go farther?

The problem is that the minimum amount of work required in order to qualify for the benefit is low and does not increase over time. Furthermore, the effective marginal tax rate is generally very high. This is exacerbated because working tax credit sits alongside a variety of unconditional benefits which neutralise its effect.

The solution would be to blend the unconditional transfers into working tax credit, and raise the minimum number of working hours required over time. The universal credit, however, will move in the opposite direction. Under the universal credit, the minimum working hours requirement is given up entirely. In theory, a universal credit recipient could permanently settle with a one-day workweek, receiving the full (or almost the full) amount of universal credit plus some additional earnings for the very short workweek. Past experience with work-contingent in-work credits shows that it does matter where the threshold is set, because many recipients tend to cluster just above.

In-work support should promote high work levels, not just entry into the labour market. This could be best achieved in the framework of the negative income tax described earlier. This should replace universal credit and also child benefit and other payments that can be received while in work. It should be conditional on a minimum number of hours worked per week, and that minimum should gradually be raised towards a level not too far away from full-time work. The requirement can be lower for those with disabilities and severe health conditions, as well as for single parents with infants. It can also be lower for those just (re-) entering the labour market. A near-full-time workload should be the standard requirement for the receipt of support, and it should apply to most people most of the time. Part of the fiscal savings achieved in this way could be recycled into a lower effective marginal tax rate, which should be no higher than the sum of the basic rate of income tax and the standard rate of national insurance.

This system would be most generous to those who put in a large number of working hours, but who can attain only a low hourly rate of pay. It would be built on the assumption that people have little control over the hourly wage they can attain, but some degree of control over the number of hours they work, even if not immediately and not all the time.

From resentment to reciprocity

Public attitudes to welfare and poverty

As explained earlier, based on macro-variables of social policy (for example, overall social expenditure), the UK has become indistinguishable from the traditionally social democratic nations. But while it is possible to import other countries' tax and welfare policies, importing the underlying political culture is less straightforward. Peter Saunders (2001: 29–30) describes this conflict:

> In the 'Anglo' countries, welfare reform is about more than just cutting costs. There is a widespread recognition in these countries that long-term welfare dependency is a social as well as an economic problem. The belief is that dependency on state support corrodes individuals' self-respect and represents a threat to social cohesion. These sorts of arguments are rarely heard in the Benelux countries or Scandinavia.

He concludes: 'Social democratic welfare regimes based on generous entitlements [...] are probably only sustainable in countries with relatively strong collectivistic cultures.'

This may sound like an exaggeration at first sight, but it is a consistent finding that the British welfare state generates much more resentment and negative attitudes towards recipients than its counterparts in traditional social democracies. For example, international surveys show that, in the latter countries, poverty is almost never attributed to characteristics or behaviours of poor individuals (Sefton et al., 2009: 237–42). A very different picture emerges for the UK. The 2011 British Social Attitudes Survey (BSA) asked respondents what they believe to be the main cause of child poverty. The survey offers a list of options, which have been split into three distinct groups in Table 34. One set of reasons refers to characteristics of the individuals concerned and another to structural factors entirely out of people's control. The other options are somewhat ambiguous: they cannot be classified without knowing exactly how the respondent interprets the statement. But what becomes clear is that most respondents choose individual rather than structural explanations. Even if the ambiguous options were all added to the 'structural' category, there would be a parity of individual and structural explanations.

Table 34 **Public perceptions of the causes of child poverty**[3]

Individual	Alcohol or drug abuse, unwillingness to work, family breakdown, too many children	47%
Structural	Wages too low, inequalities, benefits too low, long-term illness or disability, discrimination, lack of affordable housing	23%
Ambiguous	Lack of education, long-term worklessness, area effect, intergenerational effect, workload too low	25%

Source: NatCent Social Research (2011: 169–70)

Other volumes of the survey complement this picture, showing low levels of support for many types of welfare spending,

3   Most respondents give a nuanced answer, picking on average six responses (Nat-Cent Social Research, 2011: 169). In this version of the question, people have been asked to give what they see as the *main* reason.

widespread negative views of their recipients, and strong support for benefit cuts (see NatCent Social Research, 2010, 2009; Sefton et al., 2009: 237–42). It is inconceivable that a survey in, say, Sweden or Germany would deliver such results.[4] As similar as north-western European societies may be in so many other regards, attitudes on welfare and poverty remain different.

For poverty campaigners and those sharing their ideas, this is a never-ending source of frustration. Their explanation is effectively that the public has simply been tricked by the media and populist politicians into believing there is widespread welfare abuse. The latter are accused of deliberately creating resentment in order to distract the public from the 'real' issues. It amounts to 'stirring up those on quite low incomes against those on very low incomes, dividing and ruling, distracting from the lifestyle of the rulers'.[5] In this perspective, there are no legitimate worries about misuse of the welfare system; there are only engineered panics, ignorance and bigotry.

This is a shame because the cross-country differences in public attitudes do *not* indicate differences in sympathy for the poor, or in willingness to help. They indicate only lower tolerance towards free-riding behaviour in the UK, and greater fears of being taken advantage of. The architecture of welfare states ought to reflect such differences, if it is to go with the grain of public attitudes. It is, of course, possible for policymakers to dismiss public attitudes as bigoted and ignorant, and extend unconditional welfare

---

4   One survey in Germany showed that 43 per cent considered welfare benefits too low, 40 per cent considered them adequate, and only 13 per cent thought they were too high (Focus, 'Focus-Umfrage: Meinung zu Hartz IV gespalten', 6 February 2010).

5   Polly Toynbee, 'Cameron's big cut "idea" will only backfire on the Tories', *Guardian*, 25 June 2012.

spending anyway. But it should not come as a surprise if this breeds resentment and hostility.

Evidence from time use surveys

The poverty campaigners' work on this topic is unhelpful, mostly consisting of awkward attempts to talk up and romanticise welfare dependency. Veit-Wilson (2007: 5), for example, argues:

> Everyone in society is dependent on others;
> interdependency is the basis of all social life, everywhere and at all times. Better-off and rich people are dependent on low-paid people to do the dirty work for them. It is ignorant to claim that only social assistance recipients are 'dependent'.

This is, of course, mere sophistry, which confuses 'independence' with 'autarky' and relationships of dependence that arise as a result of free decisions in a complex economic order with those that do not. Oxfam (2010d: 11), meanwhile, attempts to portray welfare recipients as under-appreciated pillars of community life:

> Public attitudes towards people living in poverty, or on benefits, which see them as taking from society and never giving, are unfounded and unfair. [...] they ignore the huge contribution which people in poverty make through unpaid, largely invisible, work in their homes and communities. [...] Our economic system is based on measuring and valuing work, but it only measures paid work. As far as GDP and GNP are concerned, unpaid work doesn't count.

The Oxfam report describes welfare recipients as an underground army of informal volunteers:

> Whether or not they call themselves volunteers (or fulfil
> government criteria for a volunteer), people on low incomes
> who help others in their community, for no financial gain,
> play a vital role in the regeneration of some of the UK's most
> deprived areas and improve the lives of some of its most
> vulnerable people. This is what Susan Himmelweit calls
> 'maintenance of the social fabric'; it keeps a community
> functioning. (Ibid.: 17)

But while the case studies presented by Oxfam are, beyond doubt, authentic, they are just that: individual cases, just like the tabloid press depiction of 'welfare scroungers' which Oxfam and other poverty campaigners are so upset about. The Oxfam authors recognise that, according to every available figure on volunteering and civic activism, their case studies are as unrepresentative as can be. This is why a considerable part of their report has to be dedicated to explaining the discrepancy away, through speculations such as: 'Perhaps those with a lower socio-economic status are simply not confident that their skills would be valued by the voluntary sector' (ibid.: 16–17). The authors insist that welfare recipients' volunteering activities merely take different forms, but in order to arrive at that conclusion, they have to stretch their definitions of 'volunteering' very far indeed:

> [A]s Colin Williams reports, the General Household Survey
> of 2000 found that 'although just 7 per cent of unemployed
> respondents ... had been actively involved in a local
> organisation in the past three years, 67 per cent had done a
> favour for a neighbour in the previous six months'. (Ibid.: 16)

If we want to obtain a realistic picture of what constitutes a typical daily routine in neighbourhoods with high levels of worklessness, it is wholly unnecessary to rely on selected case studies, anecdotes or clichés. There are extensive surveys documenting how people with various socio-economic characteristics allocate their time between different activities – according to *their own* account. The Centre for Time Use Research at Oxford University provides the Multinational Time Use Study (MTUS), and Eurostat provides the Harmonized European Time Use Survey (HETUS). A paper by Krueger and Mueller (2008a) draws on these data sets to explore differences in the daily routines of the unemployed and the employed population. Their data for the UK are from 2000/01, a boom year with very low unemployment, which is an important caveat to be borne in mind.

A particular focus of the study is the average amount of time the unemployed dedicate to seeking work. The survey's definition of 'job search' is not exhaustive, but quite extensive: reading and replying to job advertisements, updating a CV, calling or visiting a labour office or agency, job interviews, and working on a portfolio. In the UK, work search activities among the unemployed took up between six and eight minutes per day on average. This is an extremely skewed average which is not in itself meaningful to interpret. It is the result of 86–90 per cent of the respondents declaring not having looked for work at all on the respective day, while the remaining 10–14 per cent have spent considerable time looking for work.

Time spent on other activities is reported only for an average of seven western European countries, not for the UK separately. But in so far as data is available for the individual country level, the difference between the UK and the western European average does not seem to be too large, so the European figures can also be considered ballpark figures for the UK. They are presented in Table 35, referring to weekdays only.

Table 35 **Evidence from time-use surveys: minutes per weekday spent on selected activities, employed and unemployed respondents, western Europe[6]**

	Employed	Unemployed
Work	395	19
Job search	0	14
Education	7	25
Voluntary, religious and civic activities	6	9
Home production and care of others	120	224
Sleeping, eating, shopping, sports	596	698
Watching TV, socialising, leisure activities	179	313

Source: Based on data from Krueger and Mueller (2008a: 28)

In Krueger's and Mueller's summary: 'In each region, the unemployed sleep substantially more than the employed. [...] The unemployed spend considerably more time than the employed in leisure and social activities. A large share of this difference is due to TV watching' (ibid.: 7–8).

The figures need to be treated with great caution. As already mentioned, the British figures refer to a boom year with very low unemployment, and would surely look very different today. The sample size and time period covered are limited and the data cannot show why people who have not looked for work have not done so. Some may have given up searching for work, after having searched extensively in the past. Some may have been looking for work in different ways, which would not count as classic work search activities. For example, one could interpret education as a work-focused activity, and add the minutes of that category to job search.

---

6   The western European countries are Austria, Belgium, France, Germany, Italy, Spain and the UK.

But with all these caveats in mind, the figures represent a vastly more authentic impression of welfare dependency than the romanticised image construed by the poverty campaigners. They are self-reported, and there is no reason why the unemployed should under-report their own work search efforts.[7] 'Scrounger-phobia' is both unjustified and unhelpful. But so is the poverty campaigners' refusal to take public concerns about welfare seriously, and their determination to cling to what Murray (1990: 67–8) calls 'a sort of modern Rousseauism in which the noble savage is replaced by the noble poor person'.

Working with the grain: the importance of reciprocity in welfare

Attitudes towards welfare may differ substantially even across otherwise similar countries, but the basic determinants of solidarity and willingness to help are understood well enough. An interesting summary of the quantitative and qualitative research is provided by Horton and Gregory (2009: 110–30). It shows, first of all, that most people are not indifferent to the distress of others. Most people, however, have strong views on what they expect from those receiving help. The single biggest deterrent to generosity is fear of being taken advantage of. Free-riding is so destructive that it need not even be especially widespread in order to undermine people's willingness to help. At the same time, nothing boosts the willingness to be generous as much as the confidence that most recipients of aid will collaborate, and do their best to improve their own situation.

---

7   If anything, some socially desirable activities have been found to be over-reported in time use surveys (Brenner, 2009).

The bottom line of the research is that people empathise with those who try – even if they try unsuccessfully. This is such a strong determinant of people's willingness to help others that it trumps all other considerations.

An interesting illustration is an experimental study in which participants are presented with a set of fictional characters, and are asked to evaluate the degree to which they are deserving (ibid.: 123–30). One of the characters has entered hard times through no fault of his own, receives benefits now, has the opportunity to change his situation, but does not do so. Another character has only himself to blame for having come on hard times, but is now doing his best to get his life back on track again. Participants empathised more strongly with the latter character. People are not primarily interested in who is to blame for a situation, but in who is doing their best to remedy the situation.

One could view the findings of these attitude studies as just a special case of the general findings on cooperative behaviour and reciprocity from behavioural economics. The basic outline of experimental studies in this field is as follows: participants play a game in which the rules are set in such a way that cooperation leads to higher overall rewards, but each individual has an incentive to free-ride on the cooperative behaviour of others (see Haidt, 2012: 178–81). Most people start with a cooperative attitude – not because of the financial incentives, but because this is their sense of what is fair and proper. There is usually a small number of free-riders, however. As the game proceeds through several rounds, the overall level of cooperation declines. Even those who start the game with a high willingness to cooperate are so upset by the free-riders that they gradually cut back their own contributions. Then, a crucial new element is introduced: the possibility to punish free-riders, by taking some of their gains away. This possibility is used extensively, and the initial level of cooperativeness is quickly restored. In later rounds, punishments are rarely used. The threat that they could be used is enough to keep free-riders at bay.

In this sense, welfare can be seen as merely a special application: special insofar as most 'players' know that, on a lifetime basis, they will be net contributors. They do not 'play' for their own benefit, so they have an even greater reason to expect a willingness to cooperate from those they help.

The policy implication from these insights is not that welfare payments should be meagre, but that they should be conditional. They should come with sensible requirements, and swift sanctions for non-compliance. Welfare payments can be generous, if they come with the right strings attached. That is the way to deal with poverty and encourage the behaviour that will keep people out of poverty.

A denationalisation of welfare

The anti-workfare coalition

We have already discussed the importance of work incentives, and proposed a way to improve them. One qualification has to be made, however. Incentives matter for those who are not far detached from the labour market. Incentives to progress in the labour market matter for those who are already in minor employment and for whom taking on more hours makes no financial sense. Incentives to enter the labour market matter for those who could do so without major difficulties and who would do so if it was more lucrative (Brewer and Browne, 2006). But incentives matter much less for those who are cut adrift from the world of

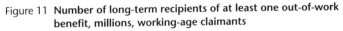

Figure 11 **Number of long-term recipients of at least one out-of-work benefit, millions, working-age claimants**

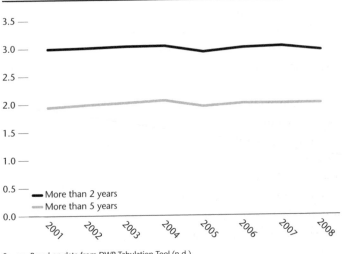

Source: Based on data from DWP Tabulation Tool (n.d.)

work. About two million working-age adults have been claiming out-of-work benefits for more than five years, a share which has been remarkably constant over the past decade (DWP Tabulation Tool, n.d.) – see Figure 11.[8] They are very unlikely to be mobilised by a change in the replacement rate, whether it comes from a change in the denominator or the numerator.

In recent years, a potential solution that has been more widely discussed is workfare. In the UK, workfare schemes are

---

8   The key benefits are income support, jobseekers' allowance, employment and support allowance (previously incapacity benefit), disability living allowance and severe disablement allowance. Two million is not the sum of the claimant counts, which would be much higher because of the overlap, i.e. claimants receiving more than one benefit.

small. There are programmes that contain certain workfare elements, but their coverage is low, and most recipients of out-of-work benefits will never have heard of them. Nevertheless, the term 'workfare' has become tainted already. The controversies surrounding the government's work experience programme (WEP), as well as the fraud scandals surrounding the employment agency A4e, have left their mark.[9]

The work experience programme is not truly a workfare programme since participation is entirely voluntary. Under this scheme, recipients of jobseekers' allowance have the option of working for a private sector employer for a short period without pay, but without a reduction in jobseekers' allowance. The rationale is to open an additional route in the job search process: for those who have already written a large number of unsuccessful applications, the 'marginal benefit' of writing another one may be small compared with an activity that enables them to signal work-related habits.

The programme led to the spontaneous formation of vociferous protest groups, which denounced the scheme as 'slave labour'. Fearing reputational damage, several large companies pulled out, leading the programme's opponents to declare victory:

> Protest works! With the right action on the right issue at
> the right place and time, a small band of people can win
> the day [...] No use demonstrating outside the Department
> for Work and Pensions, but companies are highly sensitive
> about their image. [...] So, what a joy to see the rapid retreat
> of others from workfare – Sainsbury's, Waterstones and
> Matalan among the fastest to escape.[10]

---

9   In the media coverage, A4e was often referred to as 'a private workfare provider' or 'welfare-to-work provider'.
10 Polly Toynbee, 'Protest really does work – just look at Tesco and workfare', *Guardian*, 22 February 2012.

The work experience programme is at best ersatz workfare, but it has nevertheless opened a wider debate about the concept as a whole. Opponents were quick to declare workfare an abject failure. The evidence to which they kept referring was a comparative study commissioned by the Department for Work and Pensions (DWP) (see Crisp and Fletcher, 2008), which the protest group Boycott Workfare summarised as follows: 'Research for the DWP on workfare concluded that [...] workfare has been a failure wherever it has been implemented.'[11] The *Guardian* also argued: 'The DWP has wilfully ignored comparative research it commissioned that found the model to be counter-productive.'[12] The political blog Left Foot Forward added: '[W]orkfare simply does not work. A DWP report confirms this.'[13] Finally, Cait Reilly, who took legal action against the government on the grounds that the work experience programme constituted slave labour and was thus in breach of the Human Rights Act, argued:

> Similar schemes have not worked in other countries [...] The Department for Work and Pensions hired experts to find whether 'work for your benefit' schemes delivered benefits. After studying similar programmes in Canada, the US and Australia, they found no evidence such schemes increased the chances of gaining employment.[14]

11 'Workfare does not work', Boycott Workfare, n.d.
12 'In the workfare state, poverty is always an individual failing', *Guardian*, 11 June 2009.
13 'The government's got big plans for workfare – don't expect them to back down easily', Left Foot Forward, 27 February 2012.
14 Cait Reilly, 'Why the government was wrong to make me work in Poundland for free', *Guardian*, 15 January 2012.

The workfare showcase: Wisconsin

The choir of critics, who confidently declared the failure of workfare, has probably surprised supporters of the concept, who have so far thought that the evidence was on their side. Most of the research on workfare had concentrated on the pioneer case study, Wisconsin, and came up with supportive conclusions on the whole.

Workfare reforms in Wisconsin had started cautiously in the mid-1980s, and accelerated in 1994. Today, most able-bodied welfare recipients are required to engage in work-related activities in return for their benefits, and failure to participate is sanctioned through a proportionate reduction in payments. What makes Wisconsin stand out from other states is the degree to which these work requirements have actually been enforced on the ground, rather than just existing on paper. In theory, with the 1996 Personal Responsibility and Work Opportunity Act, work requirements have become commonplace across the USA. But participation in work activities varies a lot across states. Only in eighteen states does the participation rate exceed 40 per cent of welfare recipients. Some of the most populous states, including California, Texas and Pennsylvania, record particularly low rates. Wisconsin, in contrast, achieves a participation rate of 73 per cent (Mead, 2004: 6). Wisconsin has also stood out in the actual application, rather than just the threat, of sanctions for non-participation.

Between 1994 and 2001, welfare rolls fell by 82 per cent. The vast majority of those who left the welfare rolls entered employment, often full-time (ibid.: 5, 198–200). Sanctions for non-compliance with work requirements turned out to be an effective deterrent. As many as 71 per cent of those subject to a sanction complied in the month afterwards, rather than incurring a second sanction, and subsequently had their entitlement fully restored (Wu et al., 2004).

A number of caveats have to be borne in mind when interpreting the Wisconsin experience. First of all, the decline in welfare rolls happened during a boom period with strong labour market performance. Supporters argued that previous boom periods had not witnessed comparable declines in welfare rolls, but this does not mean that the boom has not greatly enhanced the reform's potential. Secondly, the reform's impact on poverty was limited. The absolute poverty rate fell by a few percentage points, but this is far from spectacular during a boom period. More generally, Wisconsin was also a relatively easy test case: it had always been an economically and socially successful state, scoring high on measures of economic performance, social capital and institutional quality. Much of its welfare dependency and related social problems were confined to inner-city Milwaukee. But with all this in mind, a strong case for workfare still remains. So how does the workfare-critical Department for Work and Pension study fit in?

The Department for Work and Pensions report on workfare: the devil in the detail

The DWP study makes a valuable contribution to the workfare debate. It can be interpreted as an effective cautioning against a naive workfare enthusiasm. Workfare has become an increasingly broad term, comprising programmes which may look similar at first sight, but which may work very differently in practice. Not all of them are equally successful.

Some aspects of the report are questionable. The report judges a workfare scheme's success primarily by the share of recipients it manages to place into employment, their income situation after a period in work, and the duration of employment. This is sensible in principle, but unless complemented by some background information, it can lead to serious misunderstandings. A simple example can illustrate why.

Suppose there is a hypothetical welfare system with twelve recipients. Six of them are readily employable, able to hold a job, and climb up the pay scale in a reasonable timeframe. Three of them are also employable, but with greater difficulties. They will find it harder to hold a job once they have one, and their earnings potential will remain limited for the time being. The remaining three are not currently employable. They can be gradually prepared for work, but enabling them to actually hold a job and progress in it will take time. Now suppose a functioning workfare scheme is introduced. In the first year, the six most employable ones exit welfare and enter employment. They leave the system for good, and attain reasonable wages after a while. So for the first year, when judged by the DWP report's criteria, the system's performance is excellent.

But the lowest-hanging fruit has now been picked, and it will not return: since a workfare system has a greater deterrent effect than unconditional welfare, readily employable people will no longer sign up in the first place. In the second year, the three who are employable but with greater difficulties are placed into jobs. One of those loses the job and returns to workfare after a year, another one holds the job but remains on low pay for a while, while only the third one stays in work and progresses. According to the DWP report's criteria, the system's performance will still look acceptable, but not nearly as favourable as in the first year. In the third year, it will decline again.

This mechanism has to be borne in mind when reading passages such as:

> [P]articipation in W-2 [Wisconsin's workfare programme] does not lead to sustained employment in unsubsidised work for the majority of participants. Although between one-half and two-thirds of leavers found unsubsidised work at some point in each of the three years after welfare, less than half were continuously employed in this period [...] [A]pproximately half of those leaving W-2 had incomes below the poverty line. (Crisp and Fletcher, 2008: 10)

These figures do not sound impressive. But they would appear in a completely different light if the DWP report had provided some background information. Caseloads in Wisconsin began to decline in the mid-1980s when first steps towards a workfare system were taken, stagnated in the early 1990s, and then nose-dived. The system ended up with a much smaller caseload, stripped down to the most disadvantaged hard core:

> [A]s the state drove the rolls down, the more employable cases left soonest, and the demographics of the remaining cases was transformed [...] Wisconsin had driven the cream of its caseload off the rolls long before the national vogue for serious welfare reform began in the mid-1990s. But despite this, in leaver studies from the late 1990s the state attains economic outcomes on a par with those in other states, along with unusual work levels. (Mead, 2004: 210)

The omission of such background information subtracts from the report's credibility. On balance, it still remains an important contribution. But to see where exactly the report's main contribution lies, it is necessary to take a closer look at its terminological 'small print'.

In the UK, the terms 'workfare' and 'welfare to work' have generally been used as synonyms. They describe welfare systems in which the receipt of benefit payments is conditional on partici-pation in work-related activities. 'Work-related activity' can mean a number of different things. It typically includes commu-nity work, subsidised work placements, supervised job search, training, preparation for job interviews, etc. The terms 'workfare' and 'welfare to work' generally denote the whole package of activi-ties, rather than any one particular element within it. The defining feature of workfare/welfare-to-work is conditionality – mandatory participation, with the threat of a reduction in welfare payments. This is also the way in which the terms have been used in this monograph.

The DWP study, however, deviates very much from this usage, because it does not use the terms 'welfare to work' and 'workfare' as synonyms. The DWP uses 'welfare to work' as an umbrella term which refers to the whole bundle of activities that it might be feasible to include under such an arrangement, and 'workfare' as just one subcategory within it: community work. The workfare opponents make a huge mistake in citing this report as evidence for their position. The DWP report is not a critique of conditional welfare systems. It is a critique of an over-reliance on the commu-nity work component. It does not argue for an abandonment of conditional welfare, but for a rearrangement of the work-related activities, with less emphasis on community work and more emphasis on subsidised work placements. It argues that the latter are run within the labour market rather than alongside, so that participants are in closer proximity to the world of work, and more likely to acquire relevant skills. Work experience schemes, the report argues, have achieved higher rates of transition into unsubsidised employment than community work schemes.

But, in a conditional welfare system, participation in subsidised work placements in the private sector is just as mandatory as participation in community work schemes, and non-compliance is sanctioned in the same way. Thus, if community work represents 'slave labour', as it does for the British workfare opponents, then so do mandatory work placements in the private sector. The workfare opponents are not doing themselves a favour by endorsing a report which merely argues that the 'slaves' should be shifted to a different activity.

The case for denationalisation

The real lesson to take home from the DWP study is that workfare can degenerate into a bureaucratic box-ticking exercise, which places participants into some activity, but not necessarily the one which suits their needs. A Whitehall-run 'National Workfare Service' would almost certainly be like this. It would become just another target-driven, sclerotic, dysfunctional behemoth. It would be permanently in the news for incidences of mismanagement, incompetence, demotivated staff placing participants into the wrong programme tiers, etc. Politicians would blame the management culture or underfunding, and promise to 'make it better' and to 'put users in charge', but this would be just as much a chimera as promises to improve the existing large-scale bureaucracies. They cannot be 'made better'. They can only be broken up.

If workfare is going to help the poor, there should be a complete denationalisation. Local authorities should be responsible for running their own welfare systems, and fund them from locally raised taxes (similar, in some ways, to the system that existed until the 1920s). There would be no single welfare system any more, but hundreds of different ones. Local authorities would be completely free to devise their own transfer instruments, and set any eligibility criteria and conditions they see fit. A basic fiscal adjustment mechanism should ensure that even the weakest communities have the financial resources to organise a welfare system, but this adjustment should follow a standard formula reflecting local demographics and economic conditions – not actual outcomes.

This would all mean that local authorities delivering poor outcomes would not be able to pass the costs on to others. They would have to raise local taxes, and answer to local residents for their failure. If the cost of poor performance can be hidden by collectivising it, a localised welfare system would offer no advantage over the current system. If local authorities are financially accountable for their performance they are more likely to learn from best practice elsewhere, experiment with innovative approaches and draw on unique local knowledge. A localised welfare system would generate a wealth of knowledge about what works and what does not work in local circumstances. The problems faced by long-term welfare claimants in Glasgow are not the same as those faced by long-term welfare claimants in Horsham. Only full fiscal transparency would place local decision-makers under sufficient pressure from their electorates to make use of these opportunities.

This would lead to an evolutionary mechanism of constant learning and incremental improvement. Political processes cannot imitate the discovery process of markets, but a strictly local system would come reasonably close. Knowing all the ways in which central planning goes wrong and large bureaucracies fail to deliver, it is an irony that we continue to entrust the most disadvantaged members of society to this failed model.

10 CONCLUSIONS

Social expenditure in the UK stands at one of the highest levels in the world. In terms of overall social spending, the UK has overtaken traditionally social democratic nations such as the Netherlands, Norway and Finland. In terms of family benefits (spending on items such as child tax credit, child benefit, childcare subsidies, etc.) the UK has overtaken all of the Nordic countries. About 70 per cent of all children now live in a household which receives at least one type of cash benefit in addition to the quasi-universal child benefit.[1]

The outcomes from these policies are not particularly impressive. Up to a point, there clearly has been progress in reducing poverty. According to a variety of indicators, living standards among the least well off are considerably higher today than they were in the mid-1990s. But progress stalled several years before the recession and has not been revived. Whatever role the increases in transfer spending may have played in the recent past, reviving and sustaining progress in the future requires moving beyond this agenda.

The impulses and ideas for an anti-poverty agenda beyond the state-centred approach cannot come from within the current poverty lobby. The poverty lobby has proved structurally

---

1 The actual number may be higher because the HBAI survey records only the most common types of benefits, not the less well-known ones.

incapable of moving on from the mindset which inspired the anti-poverty policies of the past. They refuse to acknowledge the extent to which their traditional demands have long been met, and continue to insist on more of the same. Their programme is simply to resume the social policies of the expansionary period, and continue them indefinitely – except with an even weaker emphasis on employment and an even lower level of conditionality. Alternative strategies are either ignored or viewed with suspicion.

This is a shame because the UK's exceptionally high cost of living, as far as some of the basic essentials are concerned, is a very real issue. It is one of the main reasons why redistributive spending has been at best temporarily effective, and certainly never cost-effective. As long as the cost of some basic necessities is as exorbitant as it is currently, no amount of redistributive spending is ever going to deliver.

But the same argument also holds in reverse, and this should be the central tenet of an alternative approach to poverty alleviation. The best insurance against poverty is a product market structure in which the basic necessities of life are easily affordable right across the income distribution. There is a lot of room for legitimate disagreement about how best to achieve this aim, and about what else is required beyond that. But, in principle, this could become common ground in the poverty debate. To those who are concerned about the side effects and unintended consequences of large-scale income transfer programmes, this approach will appeal immediately. But even those who do not share these concerns will probably agree about the desirability of a situation in which such programmes are simply less necessary.

While some price developments are driven by factors outside

means that the living standards of low earners will always be a political football. Affordable prices for necessities, in contrast, are not the result of the kindness of producers; they are the result of producers' self-interested behaviour under competitive conditions. Once established, these conditions can maintain themselves, without perpetual 'Action Teams' and 'Action Zones'.

Thirdly, even if high transfer payments could insulate low earners from high basic living costs, they undermine work incentives. The British Social Attitudes Survey regularly asks participants whether they think benefit levels are too low and therefore cause hardship, or whether they think benefit levels are too high and therefore discourage work. This is an entirely false dichotomy. Ironically, both of these two statements are correct. Benefit levels are too high and discourage work, but the reason is not that they provide comfortable living standards. Benefit levels are high because they are, directly or indirectly, pegged to the basic cost of living. If the latter spirals out of control, so does the former. This does not raise their recipients' living standards, but it decreases the difference in disposable income between the workless and the low-paid. The last government tried to treat this symptom by raising in-work benefits and making more out-of-work benefits 'portable' into employment. But this has only spread the problem out farther along the income spectrum, especially for families with children. The higher the amount of benefits, the steeper the withdrawal rates have to be, in order to maintain at least some degree of targeting. But this results in high effective marginal tax and benefit withdrawal rates. Those currently outside the labour market are discouraged from entering; those working for a small number of hours are discouraged from extending their workweek. As long as the basic cost of living is anywhere near its present level, attempts to raise work levels through changes in the tax and benefit system will be like pushing water uphill.

Pro-poor policy – the impact of market reforms

The reform agenda described in this monograph would slash the basic cost of living. It is not possible to accurately assess the extent of the reduction, because the agenda has been described in broad principles, while the impact on costs would depend on many specific factors as well as many unknowns. It is possible to use a numerical example for illustrative purposes, however, providing a rough impression of what the pursuit of this policy could mean in practice.

Table 36 shows the expenditure profile of a family of four, living in a rented two-bedroom flat in a medium-sized English city such as Bristol or Milton Keynes. The rent levels in these cities are among the pricier ones, but a far cry from the likes of Brighton, Oxford, Reading or Slough, not to mention Greater London (see Table 10). The figures for spending on food, energy and childcare have been taken from the Joseph Rowntree Foundation's minimum income standard (see Davis et al., 2012), which is a hypothetical family budget produced through focus group discussions. It is, arguably, a misnomer, because the minimum income standard does not represent a 'minimum' at all, but a rather comfortable living standard. It is almost 80 per cent of median income for most family types, which means that about one third of the population falls short of it. But it is nevertheless useful for the purposes of this monograph, which is not limited to discussing living standards at the very bottom. Payments of alcohol and tobacco duties are as described in Chapter 7, corrected for under-reporting.

As explained in Chapter 3, the long-term average of the median multiple house price has been just below three. Returning median multiples to this level (say 2.9) would require a fall in average house prices of 43 per cent, given current median incomes. If this could be achieved, rent levels would follow, as they have always tracked house prices over time. This is a modest aim. As recently as the early 1980s, the average house price was no more than 2.7 times the average homebuyer's annual income, and there is no reason why this ratio should not have fallen much farther still in a more rational planning system. Median multiples have long displayed values of just below three, but this is not because a law of nature has fixed them in this region. The relatively constant long-term median multiple simply shows that the income elasticity of housing demand must have been in the vicinity of 1 for a while: as people grew wealthier, they chose to spend proportionally more on housing space and comfort, thus increasing the median house price. But it is clear that this mechanism must eventually wear off, as indeed it already has in some places. In Switzerland and Germany, for example, real-term house prices are still at about the same level as in 1970, implying falling median multiples. This should be the 'normal' long-term trajectory: rising median incomes, combined with constant or minimally rising median house prices, producing a steady decline in median multiples. In this sense, a return to median multiples of just below three should be seen as an unambitious intermediary aim. It should be noted that the long-term median multiple of three is a function itself of the post-war planning system, not of some kind of 'free for all' which involved unlimited building everywhere.

The way to achieve a fall in house prices is to liberalise the land-use planning system. Space is not an issue. There is more developable land in the UK than could ever be built upon, and without even getting near attractive natural landscapes. But any government which is willing to address this issue must first abandon the comfortable illusion that the housing crisis can be overcome without upsetting vociferous nimby groups. Attempts to pour more money into the housing market through targeted subsidies will simply raise housing costs if supply remains static. A pro-poor government must find the courage to actively confront the opposing lobbies and interest groups, and keep up the confrontation for a long time.

Falling commercial rents and a more rational allocation of retail space would produce falling consumer prices across the board. Table 36 contains just one isolated example of this: it shows what would happen if the cost of a standard food basket were to fall to the level observed in the Netherlands and Germany, which is 15 per cent below British levels. This aim is also far from ambitious, because food prices in these two countries are not particularly cheap. They have merely been chosen as benchmarks because of their relative similarity to the UK in terms of variables which might also affect food prices (for example, climate, income levels and population density). Food prices are just one example among many prices that affect the poor. Planning affects the retail sector as a whole, as well as every other sector that requires more than a minimum amount of space, such as the hotel and catering industries. So again, the table just provides an appetiser for what could be achieved.

As explained in Chapter 5, the price-increasing measures in the Common Agricultural Policy (CAP) currently raise EU food prices about 11 per cent above world market price levels. An abolition of the CAP would slash food prices by that amount – but this captures only the immediate and direct effect. The strongest argument in favour of abolishing the CAP is that it would allow competitive forces to reshape domestic agriculture in its entirety, and establish a whole new pattern of international division of labour. These dynamic effects are impossible to quantify.

The reduction in energy cost shown in Table 36 is, again, limited to the very tip of the iceberg. It shows what would happen to energy prices if direct measures to subsidise renewable energy through consumers' fuel bills were abolished. Not even the cost of the EU emissions trading scheme is included. It is simply assumed that the government will pursue carbon-reduction policies in a more efficient way. There is nothing intrinsically wrong with attempts to internalise the implicit cost of environmentally damaging actions through Pigouvian taxes. But their rates should be limited to some independent estimate of the relevant external cost. The aim here is not to reach precision or objectivity, which is, by the subject's very nature, impossible. The aim is to stop the current practice of using the labels 'green', 'environmental' or 'sustainable' for any policy measure to exempt it from rational debate. These labels have become all-purpose justifications.

On the whole, the preferential treatment of renewable energy has a substantial impact on the cost of living, with the direct impact on household fuel bills being only a minor fraction of the total. The policy's main effect is to raise production costs (Lewis and Taylor, 2012: 29–30), a share of which is then passed on to final consumers, even if this cannot be quantified since the pass-through rate is different for every product. Suffice it to say that the poverty campaigners' indifference to passed-on costs is an expression of what Brian Caplan calls the 'stick-it-to-the-man bias', the erroneous belief that costs like these are paid 'by industry' and therefore irrelevant. A market-based anti-poverty strategy, in contrast, cannot ignore regulation-induced costs.

There is also a possibility that the current, restrictive approach to the extraction of shale gas is partly motivated by a political desire to uphold the case for subsidising renewables. The shale gas boom in the USA has been cited as a reason why the USA has bucked the global trend of rising energy prices (ibid.). Proven reserves in the UK are not as plentiful, but they would be sufficient to lastingly transform the British energy market. The risks of shale gas extraction cannot be judged here since this is clearly a geophysical and not an economic issue. But the general principle should be that, while these risks ought to be carefully evaluated and monitored, this must be done in a comparative perspective. The relevant benchmark has to be the risks associated with other forms of energy generation. Risk evaluation must not be an excuse for protecting politically favoured industries within the energy sector.

On this issue, the least consistent position has been taken by environmental groups. On the one hand, they deem the risk of catastrophic global warming so existential that it must trump every other concern. But, at the same time, the hypothetical risk of local earth tremors caused by shale gas extraction – and shale gas is, after all, a relatively low-carbon energy source – is deemed completely unacceptable.

Something similar has happened in the field of 'sin taxes', especially with duties on alcohol and tobacco. The health risks associated with smoking and excessive drinking are now universally known and, especially in the former case, consumption has dropped dramatically over the past four decades. The prevalence of smoking has dropped from one out of two adults to one out of five, and this has changed the composition of the remaining 'stock of smokers'. Compared with the 1970s, the contemporary 'median smoker' is in a much lower income percentile and shows a much lower price elasticity of demand. This has simultaneously made the taxation of tobacco more regressive and less effective. One need not be opposed to a 'nanny state' in principle to realise that this is an unfavourable trade-off. Slashing sin taxes by, say, half is low-hanging fruit to improve the living standards of some of the least well off. It need not stop here. A good economic case can be made for the abolition of all sin taxes.

Childcare has become a luxury good, even though there is nothing inherently expensive about it, since it is neither a capital-intensive nor a high-tech sector. It is made very labour-intensive through a mandatory minimum staff-to-children ratio, which prevents the spreading of fixed costs, but this is entirely regulation induced. Regulation has turned childcare into a highly standardised and formalised profession, a process which should be reversed. To the extent that parents demand a guideline-driven structure, this will emerge at the level of the proposed childminding agencies. The government's role should be limited to general oversight and the prevention of abuse; it should not try to shape the day-to-day operations through input regulation.

Most of the large continental European countries achieve similar childcare enrolment rates among low earners, but at a cost of between a third and half of the UK level. This is true for both government and private childcare costs.

Table 36 **An illustrative example of the possible effects of market liberalisation (£ per month)**

	Status quo	Reduction		Post-reform
Rent (e.g. Bristol, Canterbury, Milton Keynes)	£625	43%	£270	£355
Food	£420	15% (due to changes in domestic policy)	£60	£320
		11% (due to changes in EU policy)	£40	
Energy	£100	13%	£13	£87
Alcohol and tobacco duties	£95 (= £28 + £67)	50%	£45	£50
Childcare	£640	50%	£320	£320
	≈£1,880		£750	≈£1,130

Who will benefit?

The conclusion from Table 36 is *not* that every family in comparable circumstances could be made at least £750 per month better off. The impact on the family's living standards would depend on the extent to which they pay for their own bills. If, for example, their housing costs were fully covered by housing benefit, they would not feel any direct improvement, because their housing benefit entitlement would decrease by the same amount as their rent. The largest beneficiaries would be those families which work, but which earn just a bit too much to qualify for significant amounts of transfer payments. Those with no income of their own would benefit least, because their benefit payments would probably be adjusted downwards to reflect the new basic living costs. But this would produce desirable dynamic effects. The gap between those in low-paid full-time employment and the workless would widen a lot, strengthening incentives to switch from the latter to the former group.

It should be noted that, given that benefits tend to be indexed to the general level of prices, the emphasis of this policy on reducing prices of goods that form a particularly high proportion of the budget of the poor will mean that, indirectly, the real incomes of people on benefits will rise (unless explicit action is taken to claw back the increase in the real value of benefits to the less well off).

Indeed, one should think of this as being a form of 'Pareto improvement'. If the poor themselves are not better off as a result of these policy changes, then there will be reductions in government spending. These reductions could be used to reduce taxes (in general or just for the less well off) or to provide higher benefits for the less well off – though that is not the preferred policy. The dynamic benefits of lower tax rates will benefit the poor too.

Millions of households are somewhere in between the two extreme situations, with both wages and state transfers representing important sources of income. This will include many pensioner households. For them, the impact of the supply-side agenda would also be somewhere in between the two extremes. They would not reap the full benefit of lower basic living costs, because part of the effect would be offset by downward adjustments in transfers. But given the potential magnitudes involved, there would still be enough left to boost their living standards considerably. Many households would also be taken out of the benefits system (because of the reduced level of housing benefit and higher real incomes), again producing beneficial dynamic effects.

We have focused on removing market distortions that drive up the cost of basic essentials such as housing, childcare, food and energy. There are many other areas – public transport and educational services come to mind – where similar arguments apply. All of these constitute areas which offer great potential for raising low earners' living standards at no cost to the taxpayer and without harmful side effects – or at least raising the quality of service for a given cost. But these policies would take us beyond the scope of this monograph.

Pro-poor policy – the need for welfare reform

The second major plank of a comprehensive anti-poverty strategy should consist of raising work levels among groups with weak labour-market attachment. Despite the poverty campaigners' insistence, work does offer a sustainable route out of poverty. But two caveats have to be kept in mind.

Workless households and the tax and benefits system

Firstly, what matters for poverty reduction is not aggregate employment rates, but the share of working-age adults and children in workless households. Increasing the number of people in the labour market will not reduce poverty if the increase consists of people entering the labour market from households that are currently quite well off. The overall employment rate in the UK is fairly high, but it masks a highly polarised employment structure with many double-earner and many zero-earner house-holds. The polarisation is strongest among households with children. At least 4.9 million children live in a household with both parents in work,[2] while 2.1 million children live in a house-hold with no parent in work. The latter corresponds to about 17 per cent of all children, which is easily the highest rate in Europe.

This polarisation of 'work-poor' and 'work-rich' households is matched by a polarised structure of work incentives. Once one partner has attained a certain earnings level, there are no grave financial disincentives which would deter a potential second earner from entering the labour market as well. Means-tested payments have generally been withdrawn already, so extra earnings will not be offset by a reduction in state support.[3] But, in a workless household, the barrier for a potential first earner is high, because this household still has all its means-tested income transfers to lose.[4] For various reasons, disincentives are strongest for households where there is only one potential earner to begin with, i.e. single-parent households.

---

2   'At least' because figures for the self-employed are not available in this format, and neither are figures for households where both parents work part-time. The actual number is probably a lot higher.

3   Indeed, there are incentives to split income between the two spouses of a married couple and these incentives will grow stronger with the government's reform to child benefit from 1 January 2013.

4   Take the case of a couple with two children where one adult earns a gross salary of, for example, £32,000. In this range, they will generally no longer qualify for tax credits or means-tested benefits. If the second partner decides to join the labour market – for example, at annual pay of £12,000 – household income will increase by almost £10,700. Compare this with the case of a workless household in receipt of universal credit, where one partner enters the labour market at the same annual pay of £12,000. Above a disregard, they will lose 65p for every £1 of net earnings and then, after the relevant allowances, also pay income tax and national insurance.

Secondly, even when measured at the household level, distinguishing only between the employment status 'in work' and 'out of work' is inadequate. Unfortunately, the current debate about the role of work in overcoming poverty is often trapped in this crude dichotomy. It might be a leftover from a time when, in most households, the main earner was either employed full-time and year-round, or not at all. But it fails to grasp how much labour-market attachment has become a continuous variable, on various dimensions. Several elements of the previous government's anti-poverty strategy, especially the introduction of the working families' tax credit and the extension of childcare provision, were aimed at encouraging labour-market entry. This is all well and good, but what has been neglected is the importance of labour-market progression: moving on from minor employment to something close to a full-time workweek, and/or from sporadic to continual employment. As many as 11 per cent of all children now live in a household where the main earner works part-time, which usually means a working week of about sixteen hours. Again, this is built in to the incentive structure of the tax and benefit system. The system currently provides a notable incentive to enter the labour market at sixteen hours a week or just above, but a strong disincentive against moving on from there. At this threshold, a payment of nearly £4,000 per year in working tax credit is mobilised, and 70 per cent of childcare costs are refunded (subject to a cap).

Once somebody is working sixteen hours per week at an hourly rate of £7.75 (or alternatively eighteen hours at £6.85), however, they have already reached the threshold beyond which working tax credit is withdrawn again. If they increase their gross earnings to the personal allowance of income tax, they lose 73p for every additional £1 of gross income.[5] Individuals have an incentive to work sixteen hours a week in order to access working families' benefits. They have little incentive to work beyond this level, however.

The coming universal credit is a huge improvement over the current bureaucratic swamp. Its greater clarity alone can be expected to improve work incentives, because, even if the rewards from working are not noticeably increased, recipients will at least know for sure what those rewards will be. The universal credit will also do away with the most absurd marginal tax and benefit withdrawal rates of 90 per cent or above that can arise when several means-tested transfers are withdrawn at once. But there are a number of problems which the UC will not address. Specifically, these are:

- Work incentives will remain polarised across households. Once one household member has attained a certain earnings level, there is no strong disincentive that would bar their partner from entering work as well, and becoming a second earner. But as long as no adult is in work, the disincentives for one adult to work are substantial. This effect is obviously most pronounced for households with only one potential earner: i.e. single parents.
- Incentives to work for a small number of hours will be

5 There are currently three separate thresholds. One is for working tax credit withdrawal; one for national insurance; and one for income tax. The effective marginal tax rate jumps from 0 per cent to 41 per cent when earnings cross the first threshold; to 53 per cent at the second threshold; and to 73 per cent at the third threshold. The thresholds are, however, close together. Other means-tested payments, such as housing benefit and council tax benefit, raise effective marginal tax rates at any level of earnings.

strengthened, but incentives to increase earnings further from there will remain weak. The most common effective marginal tax rate for universal credit recipients will be 76 per cent.

- Couple penalties will remain.
- The universal credit will do little to help those who have become so detached from the labour market that they no longer respond to incentives alone. There are a few patchy programmes with workfare elements, but their coverage and duration will be limited.

In order to promote work and progression, the system needs a complete overhaul. Universal credit merges disparate payment streams into one, but keeps most other features of the current system.

In-work benefits should be merged with income tax, which should, in turn, be merged with national insurance, into a single system of positive and negative taxation. The personal allowance should be replaced by household allowances, which should differ across household types but be equal in equivalised terms (that is, after allowing for living costs of different household sizes). Households whose combined earnings fell below their household allowance would be 'negatively taxed': i.e. they would receive a payment. Households whose combined earnings exceeded their household allowance would pay the standard 'positive income tax'. This is shown in Table 37 for a stylised example, with three different household types and three different earnings scenarios. It uses a stylised equivalence scale, which assumes that a single adult earning 65 gold coins is exactly as well off as a parental couple with two children earning 150 gold coins, and a single parent with one child earning 90 gold coins. The tax rate for both positive and negative taxation is assumed to be 32 per cent.

Table 37 **A hypothetical system of negative and positive income taxation**

		Two adults, two children	One adult, one child	Single adult
Household allowance		150	90	65
Income = 65	Tax liability	−27	−8	0
	Disposable income	92	73	65
Income = 90	Tax liability	−19	0	8
	Disposable income	109	90	82
Income = 150	Tax liability	0	19	27
	Disposable income	150	117	109

Receipt of the negative income tax (NIT) should be conditional on a minimum number of hours worked, and once a household is in work, that minimum should be raised gradually. The funds saved by requiring recipients to work for more hours make low effective marginal tax rates affordable. The basic idea is that the low-skilled may have little influence on the hourly wage rate they can attain, but more influence on the amount of working hours they put in. So the system of in-work support should be most generous to those who work long hours for low pay.

Out-of-work benefits

The system of out-of-work benefits, meanwhile, should be completely devolved to the local level. Local authorities should run their own welfare system, and fund it from local taxation.

There would be no such thing as 'the British welfare system' any more, because it would be replaced by hundreds of local welfare systems which could be completely different from one another. Overall, this polycentric system would create much more knowledge than the current monolith. It would allow innovation and experimentation while also providing feedback mechanisms for decision-makers. Different models would be benchmarked against one another, and voters would be able to hold decision-makers to account.[6]

A 'race to the bottom' is the least likely outcome; fears that voters would always vote for the 'cheapest' policy are unfounded. The evidence on the factors that drive attitudes to welfare shows that the vast majority of people are not indifferent to the distress of others. But they do have strong views on what they expect from welfare recipients. The current lack of support for many types of welfare spending, and the resentment of its recipients, does not indicate a lack of sympathy. It indicates a lack of trust in the system, as many people fear it does not require cooperation from its recipients. In a localised system, local policymakers would be under constant pressure from their electorates to keep free-riding at bay. This means that most systems emerging under those conditions would be workfare systems of one kind or another. But the flipside of the same argument is that once a system of conditionality and reciprocity was in place, local welfare systems could afford to be generous, and with public approval.

Workfare systems yield a large initial dividend as they push

---

6   A very rapid start could be made by devolution of welfare spending and the taxation authority required to finance it to Scotland, Wales and Northern Ireland. Those nations could then decide for themselves how much further to devolve authority.

the more employable cases into work quickest. It is this thinning of the welfare rolls which liberates the resources, enabling the system to concentrate on supporting the most difficult cases properly.[7]

And this is, last but not least, one of the ironies of an approach to poverty alleviation that tries to define as many people as possible as 'needy' and 'vulnerable'. Since such a system must necessarily adopt a greater level of standardisation, it must become bureaucratic and formalistic, substituting box-ticking for personalised support. The system becomes more likely to fail the more complex cases, who cannot be helped by following the rule book. There is a trade-off between a system's scope and its ability to focus on individual cases. A system which administers millions of cases cannot, at the same time, pay attention to the specifics of each case.

The market-based approach identified in this monograph will not work for everybody. There will always be people who need help and support, no matter how buoyant the labour market, and no matter how competitive the product markets. But perhaps the greatest side effect of an approach based on empowerment and independence is that it enables support systems to concentrate properly on those who need them most.

---

7   This is, to some extent, observable in the Wisconsin case study. The initial sharp decline in the welfare rolls was not matched by an equivalent decline in welfare spending. Instead, spending per recipient increased, as the support infrastructure became more comprehensive. The fiscal savings came only much later. They were a welcome by-product, not a main purpose of welfare reform.

REFERENCES

Acemoglu, D. and J. Angrist (2001), 'Consequences of employment protection? The case of the Americans with Disabilities Act', *Journal of Political Economy*, 109(5): 915–57.

Adam. S. and J. Browne (2010), 'Redistribution, work incentives and thirty years of UK tax and benefit reform', IFS Working Paper 10/24, London: Institute for Fiscal Studies.

Adam, S., M. Brewer and A. Shephard (2006), 'Financial work incentives in Britain: comparisons over time and between family types', Working Paper 06/2006, London: Institute for Fiscal Studies.

Addison, J. and P. Teixeira (2001), 'The economics of employment protection', Discussion Paper no. 381, Bonn: Institute for the Study of Labour.

Anderson, K., W. Martin and E. Valanzuela (2006), 'The relative importance of global agricultural subsidies and market access', *World Trade Review*, 5(3): 357–76.

Andrews, D., A. Caldera Sánchez and Å. Johansson (2011), 'Housing markets and structural policies in OECD countries', OECD Economics Department Working Papers no. 836, Paris: OECD Publishing.

Anthony, J. (2003), 'The effects of Florida's Growth Management Act on housing affordability', *Journal of the American Planning Association*, 69(3): 282–95.

Arthur, T. and P. Booth (2010), *Does Britain Need a Financial Regulator? Statutory regulation, private regulation and financial markets*, London: Institute of Economic Affairs.

Attanasio, O., E. Battistin and A. Leicester (2006), 'From micro to macro, from poor to rich: consumption and income in the UK and the US', Paper prepared for the conference 'The well being of families and children as measured by consumption behavior', National Poverty Center.

BBC News (2010), 'Incompetent teachers being recycled by head teachers', available at http://www.bbc.co.uk/news/10464617.

Becerra, G. (2006), 'Arancel efectivo de las importaciones chilenas', *Estudios Económicos Estadísticos*, 50, Santiago: Banco Central de Chile.

Bell, D. and A. Heitmueller (2009), 'The disability discrimination act in the UK: helping or hindering employment among the disabled?', *Journal of Health Economics*, 28(2): 465–80.

BIS (2010), 'Findings from the Survey of Employment Tribunal Applications', Employment Relations Research Series no. 107, BMRB Social Research, Department for Business, Innovation and Skills.

Blankart, C. (2007), *Föderalismus in Deutschland und Europa*, Baden-Baden: Nomos.

Blankart, C. (2008), *Öffentliche Finanzen in der Demokratie*, Munich: Franz Vahlen Verlag.

Blundell, R. (2001), 'Welfare reform for low income workers', *Oxford Economic Papers*, 53/2001: 189–214.

Brenner, P. (2009), 'Overreporting of socially desirable behavior in a cross-national perspective: religious service attendance as a sample case', Department of Sociology, Madison: University of Wisconsin–Madison.

Brewer, M. and J. Browne (2006), 'The effect of the Working Families' Tax Credit on labour market participation', IFS Briefing Note no. 69, London: Institute for Fiscal Studies.

Brewer, M. and C. O'Dea (2012), 'Measuring living standards with income and consumption: evidence from the UK', IFS Working Paper W12/12, London: Institute for Fiscal Studies.

Brewer, M. and A. Shephard (2004), 'Has Labour made work pay?', London: Institute for Fiscal Studies and Joseph Rowntree Foundation.

Brewer, M., A. Duncan, A. Shephard, M. Suarez and M. Jose (2006), 'Did working families' tax credit work? The impact of in-work support on labour supply in Great Britain', *Labour Economics*, 13: 699–720.

Brewer, M., A. Muriel, D. Philips and L. Sibieta (2008), 'Poverty and inequality in the UK 2008', IFS Commentary 105, London: Institute for Fiscal Studies.

Brewer, M., C. O'Dea, G. Paull and L. Sibieta (2009), 'The living standards of families with children reporting low incomes', Research Report no. 577, London: Institute for Fiscal Studies for the Department of Work and Pensions.

Browne, J. and G. Paull (2010), 'Parents' work entry, progression and retention, and child poverty', Research Report no. 626, prepared for the Department for Work and Pensions, London: Institute for Fiscal Studies.

Brueckner, J. (1990), 'Growth controls and land values in an open city', *Land Economics*, 66(3): 237–48.

Bundesamt für Statistik (2009), 'Bevölkerungsindikatoren nach Kantonen', Data set, Neuchatel: BfS Switzerland.

Bundesamt für Statistik (2011), 'Bevölkerungsindikatoren nach Kantonen', Data set, Neuchatel: BfS Switzerland.

Cancer Research UK (2012), *Smoking Statistics*, available at http://info.cancerresearchuk.org/cancerstats/types/lung/smoking/lung-cancer-and-smoking-statistics#percent.

Carswell, D. and D. Hannan (2008), *The Plan. Twelve months to renew Britain*, London: Douglas Carswell.

Centraal Bureau voor de Statistiek (2010), 'Ontwikkeling van de bevolking en bevolkingsdichtheid per provincie', Data set, available at http://www.compendiumvoordeleefomgeving.nl/tabellen/n1000112b.html.

Cheshire, P., C. Hilber and I. Kaplanis (2011), 'Evaluating the effects of planning policies on the retail sector: or do Town Centre First policies deliver the goods?', SERC Discussion Paper no. 66, Spatial Economics Research Centre, London School of Economics.

Chi-man Hui, E. and V. Sze-mun Ho (2002), 'Does the planning system affect housing prices? Theory and evidence from Hong Kong', Department of Building and Real Estate, Hong Kong: Hong Kong Polytechnic University.

Coote, A., J. Franklin and A. Simms (2010), *21 hours. Why a shorter working week can help us all to flourish in the 21st century*, London: New Economics Foundation.

Corkindale, J. (2004), *The Land Use Planning System*, London: Institute of Economic Affairs.

Cox, W. (2011), 'Constraints on housing supply: natural and regulatory', *Econ Journal Watch*, 8(1): 13–27.

CPAG (2005), 'Ten steps to a society free of child poverty. Child Poverty Action Group's manifesto to eradicate child poverty', London: Child Poverty Action Group.

CPAG (2006), 'Comprehensive Spending Review 207: What it needs to deliver on child poverty', CPAG Policy Briefing, London: Child Poverty Action Group.

CPAG (2008), 'No one written off. Response to the July 2008 welfare reform Green Paper', London: Child Poverty Action Group.

CPAG (2009a), 'Stop in-work poverty: end sub-prime jobs', London: Child Poverty Action Group.

CPAG (2009b), 'Ending child poverty: a manifesto for success', London: Child Poverty Action Group.

CPAG (2010a), 'Slashed housing benefit subverts the meaning of fairness', Child Poverty Action Group press release.

CPAG (2010b), 'Work: the best route out of poverty?', *Poverty*, 137: 15–17.

CPAG (2011a), 'Government faces legal challenge to housing benefit cuts', Child Poverty Action Group press release, 7 March.

CPAG (2011b), *Campaigns Newsletter*, 78, September.

CPAG (2011c), 'Court rules to allow discriminatory impacts of Housing Benefit cuts', press release, Child Poverty Action Group.

CPAG (2012), 'Tax credits calamity hammers 200,000 families and harms the economy', Press release.

CPRE (2006), *Policy-based evidence making. The Policy Exchange's war against planning*, A CPRE Report, London: Campaign to Protect Rural England.

Cribb, J., R. Joyce and D. Phillip (2012), 'Living standards, poverty and inequality in the UK: 2012', IFS Commentary C124, London: Institute for Fiscal Studies.

Crisp, R. and D. R. Fletcher (2008), 'A comparative review of workfare programmes in the United States, Canada and Australia', Research Report no. 533, London: Department for Work and Pensions.

Cugelmann, B. and E. Otero (2010), 'Evaluation of Oxfam GB's climate change campaign', Leitmotiv, AlterSPark and Oxfam GB.

Davis, A., D. Hirsch, N. Smith, J. Beckhelling and M. Padley (2012), *A Minimum Income Standard for 2012. Keeping up in hard times*, London: Joseph Rowntree Foundation.

Dawkins, C. and A. Nelson (2002), 'Urban containment policies and housing prices: an international comparison with implications for future research', *Land Use Policy*, 19: 1–12.

Dawson, G. (2008), 'The economic science fiction of climate change: a free market perspective on the Stern Review and the IPCC', *Economic Affairs*, 28(4): 42–7.

Daycare Trust (2012), *Childcare Costs Survey 2012*, London: Daycare Trust.

DCLG (2007), *Generalised Land Use Database, Statistics for England 2005*, London: Department for Communities and Local Government.

DCLG (2010), *English Housing Survey. Household report 2008–09*, London: Department for Communities and Local Government.

DCLG (2011a), *Draft National Planning Policy Framework*, London: Department for Communities and Local Government.

DCLG (2011b), 'Table 590: Mix-adjusted house price index, by region, from Q2 1968 (quarterly) and from 2002 (monthly)', data set, Department for Communities and Local Government.

DCLG (2011c), 'Public attitudes to housing in England. Report based on the results from the British Social Attitudes survey', London: Department for Communities and Local Government.

DCLG (2012), *National Planning Policy Framework*, London: Department for Communities and Local Government.

Deben, J. (2012), 'Where the money goes', in E. Wallis (ed.), *The Fairness Instinct. How we can harness public opinion to save the environment*, London: Fabian Society.

DECC (2010), 'Estimated impact of energy and climate change policies on energy prices and bills', London: Department of Energy and Climate Change.

Demographia (2012), '8th annual Demographia international housing affordability survey: 2012. Rankings for metropolitan markets', Performance Urban Planning.

Department for Transport (2012), 'Public attitudes to climate change and the impact of transport in 2011', ONS opinion survey, London: DfT.

DWP (2008), 'No one written off. Reforming welfare to reward responsibility', Green Paper/Public consultation, London: Department for Work and Pensions.

DWP (2011), 'Universal Credit Policy Briefing Note 14. Earnings disregards and tapers', London: Department for Work and Pensions.

DWP Statistics (2011), 'Benefit expenditure tables – medium term forecasts', Data set, London: Department for Work and Pensions.

DWP Tabulation Tool (n.d.), http://83.244.183.180/5pc/wa5/ tabtool_wa5.html, accessed 2012.

Economist House Price Indicators (2012), *Clicks and Mortar. Our interactive overview of global house prices and rents*, available at http://www.economist.com/blogs/freeexchange/2010/10/ global_house_prices.

EEX (2012), 'Market data, emission rights', Leipzig: European Energy Exchange, available at www.eex.com/en/Market%20 Data/Trading%20Data/Emission%20Rights.

Errazuriz, F. and E. Muchnik (1996), 'Visión crítica de la agricultura chilena y sus políticas', *Estudios Públicos*, 61(2): 141–88.

Euratex (2010), 'EU trade policy revision – Euratex position', Position paper, Euratex Commercial and Industrial Strategy.

European Commission (n.d.), 'Industrial goods, Textiles and footwear, Textiles sector', available at http://ec.europa. eu/trade/creating-opportunities/economic-sectors/ industrial-goods/textiles-and-footwear/#_texts.

Eurostat (2008), 'The social situation in the European Union 2007. Social cohesion through equal opportunities', Luxembourg: Office for Official Publications of the European Communities.

Eurostat (2009), 'What can be learned from deprivation indicators in Europe', Luxembourg: Office for Official Publications of the European Communities.

Eurostat (2010), 'Housing statistics in the European Union 2010', available at http://abonneren.rijksoverheid.nl/

media/00/66/040531/438/housing_statistics_in_the_
european_union_2010.pdf.

Eurostat (2012), 'Jobless households – children', Data set,
available at http://epp.eurostat.ec.europa.eu/tgm/table.do?t
ab=table&init=1&plugin=1&language=en&pcode=tps00181.

Evans, A. and O. Hartwich (2005), 'Unaffordable housing. Fables
and myths', London: Policy Exchange.

Evans, L. and A. Grimes (1996), 'Economic reforms in New
Zealand 1984–95: the pursuit of efficiency', *Journal of Economic
Literature*, 34(4): 1856–1902.

Feld, L., G. Kirchgässner and C. Schaltegger (2004), 'Fiscal
federalism and economic performance: evidence from
Swiss cantons', Marburg Working Papers on Economics
2004/20, Faculty of Business Administration and Economics,
Department of Economics, Philipps-Universität Marburg.

Feldstein, M. and J. Poterba (1984), 'Unemployment insurance
and reservation wages', *Journal of Public Economics*, 23(1/2):
141–67.

Francois, J., M. Manchin, H. Norberg and D. Spinanger (2007),
'Impacts of textiles and clothing sectors liberalisation on
prices', Final report, prepared for the Directorate-General for
Trade, Commission of the European Union.

Friedman, M. (1980), *Free to Choose. A personal statement*, San
Diego/New York/London: Harcourt.

Frondel, M., N. Ritter, C. Schmidt and C. Vance (2009),
'Economic impacts from the promotion of renewable energy.
The German experience', Ruhr Economic Papers no. 156,
Department of Economics, Ruhr Universität Bochum.

Garino, G. and L. Sarno (2004), 'Speculative bubbles in UK house prices: some new evidence', *Southern Economic Journal*, 70(4): 777–95.

Gay, R. and W. Wascher (1989), 'Persistence effects in labor force participation', *Eastern Economic Journal*, 15(3): 177–87.

Glaeser, E. and J. Gyourko (2003), 'The impact of building restrictions on housing affordability', *FRNBY Economic Policy Review*, 6: 21–39, Federal Reserve Bank of New York.

Glaeser, E., J. Gyourko and R. Saks (2005a), 'Why have house prices gone up?', NBER Working Paper Series no. 11129, National Bureau of Economic Research.

Glaeser. E., J. Gyourko and R. Saks (2005b), 'Why is Manhattan so expensive? Regulation and the rise in housing prices', *Journal of Law and Economics*, 48(2): 331–69.

Goldfinch, S. (2000), *Remaking New Zealand and Australian Economic Policy. Ideas, institutions and policy communities*, Wellington: Victoria University Press.

Greenhalgh, S. and J. Moss (2009), *Principles for social housing reform*, London: Localis.

Greenpeace (n.d.), 'The problem with aviation', available at http://www.greenpeace.org.uk/climate/aviation.

Gwartney, J., R. Lawson and J. Hall (2011), *Economic freedom of the world*, 2011 annual report, Vancouver: Fraser Institute.

Haidt, J. (2012), *The Righteous Mind. Why good people are divided by politics and religion*, London: Penguin.

Hartwich, M. O. and A. Evans (2005), *Unaffordable Housing, Fables and Myths*, London: Policy Exchange.

Heritage Foundation (2011), *2010 Index of Economic Freedom*, Washington, DC: Heritage Foundation.

Hilber, C. and W. Vermeulen (2010), *The impact of restricting housing supply on house prices and affordability*, final report, Department for Communities and Local Government.

Hills, J. (2007), *Ends and means: the future roles of social housing in England*, CASE Report 34, Centre for Analysis of Social Exclusion.

Hills, J., T. Sefton and K. Stewart (eds) (2009), *Towards a More Equal Society? Poverty, inequality and policy since 1997*, Bristol: Policy Press.

Hirsch, D. (2006), *What will it take to end child poverty? Firing on all cylinders*, York: Joseph Rowntree Foundation.

HM Courts and Tribunals Service and Ministry of Justice (2011a), 'Employment tribunals and EAT statistics, 2010–11', *Annual Statistics*.

HM Courts and Tribunals Service and Ministry of Justice (2011b), Data set accompanying 'Employment tribunals and EAT statistics, 2010–11', *Annual Statistics*.

HMRC (2012), 'Tax receipts and taxpayers: number of taxpayers and registered traders', Data set, available at http://www.hmrc.gov.uk/stats/tax_receipts/menu.htm.

Hoekman, B., F. Ng and M. Olarreaga (2004), 'Agricultural tariffs or subsidies: which are more important for developing economies?', *World Bank Economic Review*, 18(2): 175–204.

Hogan, J., I. Shaw and P. Berry (2004), *A review of the Australian dairy industry*, ABARE *e*Report 04.24, prepared for the Primary Industries Standing Committee Working Group on Dairy, Canberra: Australian Bureau of Agricultural and Resource Economics.

Horton, T. and J. Gregory (2009), *The Solidarity Society*, London: Fabian Society.

ICF International (2012), *An international comparison of energy and climate change policies impacting energy intensive industries in selected countries*, Final report, submitted to the Department for Business, Innovation and Skills.

Information und Technik Nordrhein-Westfalen (2011), *Bevölkerung in Nordrhein-Westfalen 2009: Bevölkerungsstand, Bevölkerungsbewegung*, Düsseldorf: IT-NRW, Abteilung Statistik.

International Energy Agency (2011), *CO_2 Emissions from Fuel Combustion. Highlights*, 2011 edn, Paris: IEA Statistics.

Jones, M. and J. Jones (2008), 'The labour market impact of the UK Disability Discrimination Act', *Bulletin of Economic Research*, 60(3): 289–306.

Joseph Rowntree Foundation (2010), 'Time to reconsider UK energy and fuel poverty policies?', Viewpoint Informing Debate, York: Joseph Rowntree Foundation.

Joskow, P. (2008), 'Lessons learned from electricity market liberalization', *Energy Journal*, Special issue: 'The future of electricity: papers in honor of David Newbery', pp. 9–42.

Kalaitzandonakes, N. (1994), 'Price protection and productivity growth', *American Journal of Agricultural Economics*, 76(4): 722–32.

Kay, L. (2010), *Escaping the poverty trap: helping people on benefits into work*, London: Policy Exchange.

Keane, M. and K. Wolpin (1997), 'The career decisions of young men', *Journal of Political Economy*, 105(3): 473–522.

King, P. (2006), *Choice and the End of Social Housing*, Hobart Paper 155, London: Institute of Economic Affairs.

Krueger, A. and A. Mueller (2008a), 'The lot of the unemployed: a time use perspective', IZA Discussion Paper no. 3490, Bonn: Institute for the Study of Labour.

Krueger, A. and A. Mueller (2008b), 'Job search and unemployment insurance: new evidence from time use data', IZA Discussion Paper no. 3667, Bonn: Institute for the Study of Labour.

Kurtz, M. (1999), 'Chile's neo-liberal revolution: incremental decisions and structural transformation, 1973–89', *Journal of Latin American Studies*, 31: 399–427.

Lawson, N. (2009), *An Appeal to Reason: A cool look at global warming*, London: Duckworth Overlook.

Layard, R., S. Nickell and R. Jackman (2005), *Unemployment. Macroeconomic performance and the labour market*, Oxford: Oxford University Press.

Left Foot Forward (2012), 'The government's got big plans for workfare – don't expect them to back down easily', Blog piece, 27 February.

Leonard, A. (2010), *Political Poetry as Discourse. Rereading John Greenleaf Whittier, Ebenezer Elliott, and hip-hop-ology*, Plymouth: Lexington Books.

Leunig, T. (2007), *In my back yard: unlocking the planning system*, policy paper, London: Centre Forum.

Leunig, T. (2009), *The right to move. A new agenda for social housing tenants*, London: Policy Exchange.

Lewis, D. and C. Taylor (2012), 'Britain's shale gas potential', Infrastructure for Business 3/2012, London: Institute of Directors.

LHA Direct (2012), 'LHA rates and LHA bedroom calculator', Local Housing Allowance, previously available at http://www.direct.gov.uk/en/Di011/DoItOnline/DG_196239#changeso.

Liberal Democrats (2011), 'Inequality', Consultation Paper 102, prepared for the Liberal Democrats Spring Conference.

Ljungqvist, L. and T. Sargent (2008), 'Two questions about European unemployment', *Econometrica*, 76(1): 1–29.

Lomborg, B. (2007), *Cool It. The sceptical environmentalist's guide to global warming*, New York: Cyan and Marshall Cavendish.

Lucas, C. (2012), 'Building solidarity at home and abroad', in E. Wallis, *The Fairness Instinct. How we can harness public opinion to save the environment*, Fabian Ideas 631, London: Fabian Society, pp. 39–46.

Maddison, A. (2008), 'Statistics on world population, GDP and per capita GDP, 1–2008 AD', Data set, http://www.ggdc.net/maddison/Historical_Statistics/horizontal-file_02–2010.xls.

Malpezzi, S. (1996), 'Housing prices, externalities, and regulation in US metropolitan areas', *Journal of Housing Research*, 7(2): 209–41.

Mead, L. (1999), 'The decline of welfare in Wisconsin', *Journal of Public Administration Research and Theory* (J-PART), 9(4): 597–622.

Mead, L. (2004), *Government Matters. Welfare reform in Wisconsin*, Princeton, NJ: Princeton University Press.

Meghir, C. and D. Phillips (2008), 'Labour supply and taxes', Working Paper 08/04, London: Institute for Fiscal Studies.

Meyer, B. D. (1990), 'Unemployment insurance and unemployment spells', *Econometrica*, 58(4): 757–82.

Monbiot, G. (2011), 'This wrecking ball is Osborne's version of sustainable development', *Guardian*, 5 September.

Morgan, P. (2007), *The War between the State and the Family. How government divides and impoverishes*, London: Institute of Economic Affairs.

Murray, C. (1990), *The Emerging British Underclass*, London: Institute of Economic Affairs.

Murray, C. (1996), *Charles Murray and the Underclass: The developing debate*, Choice in Welfare no. 33, London: Institute of Economic Affairs (Health and Welfare Unit).

Myddelton, D. R. (2007), *They Meant Well. Government project disasters*, Hobart Paper 160, London: Institute of Economic Affairs.

Nardinelli, C. (n.d.), 'Industrial revolution and the standard of living', in *Concise Encyclopedia of Economics*, 2nd edn, Library of Economics and Liberty.

NatCent Social Research (2009), *British Social Attitudes Survey 26*.

NatCent Social Research (2010), *British Social Attitudes Survey 27*.

NatCent Social Research (2011), *British Social Attitudes Survey 28*.

Nedergard, P. (2006), 'Market failures and government failures: a theoretical model of the Common Agricultural Policy', *Public Choice*, 127(3/4): 393–413.

Neumark, D. and W. Stock (2007), 'The labour market effects of sex and race discrimination laws', *Economic Enquiry*, 44(3): 385–419.

Newbery, D. (2006), 'Electricity liberalization in Britain and the evolution of market design', in F. Sioshansi and W. Pfaffenberger, *Electricity Market Reform: An International Perspective*, Amsterdam: Elsevier, pp. 109–44.

Niemietz, K. (2011), 'An analysis of the welfare cuts in the Comprehensive Spending Review and the Budget 2010', *Economic Affairs*, 31(1): 80–85.

Niskanen, W. (1968), 'The peculiar economics of bureaucracy', *American Economic Review*, 58(2): 293–305.

Nordhaus, W. (2007), 'A review of the Stern Review on the economics of climate change', *Journal of Economic Literature*, 45(3): 686–702.

NOSOSCO (2004), *Single Parents in the Nordic Countries*, Copenhagen: Nordic Social-Statistical Committee.

Nutbrown, C. (2012), *Review of early education and childcare qualifications*, interim report, Nutbrown Review, prepared for the Department of Education.

OECD (2008), 'Growing unequal? Income distribution and poverty in OECD countries', Paris: OECD Publishing.

OECD (2010a), *OECD's Producer Support Estimate and related indicators of agricultural support. Concepts, calculations, interpretation and use (The PSE Manual)*, Paris: OECD Publishing.

OECD (2010b), *Agricultural policies in OECD countries at a glance*, Paris: OECD Publishing.

OECD (2011a), *Doing better for families*, Paris: OECD Publishing.

OECD (2011b), Fiscal Decentralization Database, available at http://www.oecd.org/ctp/fiscalfederalismnetwork/oecdfiscaldecentralisationdatabase.htm.

OECD (2011c), 'Housing and the economy: policies for renovation', in OECD, *Economic Policy Reforms 2011. Going for growth*, Paris: OECD Publishing.

OECD (2012), Social Expenditure Database (SOCX), available at http://www.oecd.org/els/socialpoliciesanddata/socialexpendituredatabasesocx.htm.

OECD.StatExtracts (2012), *Agriculture and fisheries, Agricultural policy indicators, Producer and consumer support estimates.*

ONS (2003), *Family Spending. A report on the 2001–02 Expenditure and Food Survey*, Revised edn, London: Office for National Statistics.

ONS (2006), 'Regional trends – population density', no. 39, London: Office for National Statistics.

ONS (2008), Dataset accompanying the publication 'The distribution of household income 1977 to 2006/07', *Economic and Labour Market Review*, 12/2008, London: Office for National Statistics.

ONS (2010), *Family Spending, 2010 Edition. A report on the Living Costs and Food Survey 2011*, London: Office for National Statistics.

ONS (2011a), *Consumer Price Indices, November 2011: Detailed CPI and RPI Briefing Tables*, available at http://www.ons.gov.uk/ons/rel/cpi/consumer-price-indices/july-2012/cpi-and-rpi-detailed-reference-tables.xls; http://www.ons.gov.uk/ons/rel/cpi/consumer-price-indices/november-2011/cpi-and-rpi-detailed-reference-tables.xls.

ONS (2011b), 'The effects of alcohol and tobacco duties on household disposable income', London: Office for National Statistics.

ONS (2012), *Consumer Price Indices, time series*, available at http://www.ons.gov.uk/ons/rel/cpi/consumer-price-indices/march-2012/cpi-time-series-data.html.

ONS and DCLG (2010), *English Housing Survey. Household report 2008–09*, London: Department for Communities and Local Government.

ONS and DCLG (2011), *Local Authority Housing Statistics, England, 2010–11*, London: Department for Communities and Local Government.

ONS and DCLG (2012a), *English Housing Survey. Households 2010–11*, London: Department for Communities and Local Government.

ONS and DCLG (2012b), 'House building: permanent dwellings completed, by tenure', Table 241, 'Live tables on house building'.

ONS and DECC (2011a), *Annual Report on Fuel Poverty Statistics 2011*, London: Office for National Statistics and Department of Energy and Climate Change.

ONS and DECC (2011b), 'Energy statistics', Press notice, statistical press release.

ONS and DWP (2011), 'Households below average income. An analysis of the income distribution 1994/95–2009/10', London: Department for Work and Pensions.

ONS and DWP (2012a), 'Households below average income. An analysis of the income distribution 1994/95–2010/11', London: Department for Work and Pensions.

ONS and DWP (2012b), 'Housing Benefit and Council Tax Benefit statistics', July, London: Department for Work and Pensions.

ONS and HMRC (2012), 'Child and working tax credits statistics', Data set, available at http://www.hmrc.gov.uk/stats/personal-tax-credits/cwtc-quarterly-stats.htm.

Oxfam (2009), 'Oxfam Cymru supports new fuel poverty campaign', press release, Oxfam GB.

Oxfam (2010a), 'Housing Benefit cuts will make people homeless and drive them away from jobs', UK Poverty Post.

Oxfam (2010b), 'Budget 2010: cutting benefits by stealth', UK Poverty Post.

Oxfam (2010c), 'Oxfam's response to the Department for Work and Pensions consultation: 21st Century Welfare', Policy Paper.

Oxfam (2010d), 'Something for nothing. Challenging negative attitudes to people living in poverty', Oxfam Discussion Paper.

Oxfam (2011), 'When work doesn't pay. In-work poverty in the UK', Oxfam Discussion Paper.

Oxley, M., T. Brown, V. Nadin, L. Qu, L. Tummers and A. Fernandez-Maldonado (2009), *Review of European Planning Systems*, Leicester: De Montfort University.

Pennington, M. (2002), *Liberating the Land. The case for private land use planning*, London: Institute of Economic Affairs.

Pissarides, C. (1992), 'Loss of skill during unemployment and the persistence of employment shocks', *Quarterly Journal of Economics*, 107(4): 1371–91.

Pollakowski, H. and S. Wachter (1990), 'The effects of land-use constraints on housing prices', *Land Economics*, 66(3): 315–24.

Power, A. (2009), 'New Labour and unequal neighbourhoods', in J. Hills, T. Sefton and K. Stewart (eds) (2009), *Towards a More Equal Society? Poverty, inequality and policy since 1997*, Bristol: Policy Press, pp. 115–33.

Quigley, J. and L. Rosenthal (2005), 'The effects of land-use regulation on the price of housing: what do we know? What can we learn?', BPHUP working paper W04–002, Berkeley Program on Housing and Urban Policy, University of Berkeley.

Research Centre of the Flemish Government (2011), *Flanders in Figures 2011*, Brussels: Koen Verlaeckt.

Rickard, S. (2012), 'Liberating farming from the CAP', IEA Discussion Paper no. 37, London: Institute of Economic Affairs.

Saks, R. (2005), 'Job creation and housing construction: constraints on metropolitan area employment growth', Working Paper, Finance and Economics Discussion Series (FEDS), Divisions of Research and Statistics and Monetary Affairs, Washington, DC: Federal Reserve Board.

Salies, E. and C. Waddams Price (2004), 'Charges, cost and market power: the deregulated UK electricity retail market', *Energy Journal*, 25(3): 19–37.

Sandrey, R. and G. Scobie (1994), 'Changing international competitiveness and trade: recent experience in New Zealand agriculture', *American Journal of Agricultural Economics*, 76(5): 1041–6.

Saunders, P. (2001), 'Australia is not Sweden. National cultures and the welfare state', *Policy*, 17(3): 29–32.

Saunders, P. and K. Tsumori (2002), *Poverty in Australia. Beyond the rhetoric*, CIS Policy Monograph 57, St Leonard's: Centre for Independent Studies.

Sefton, T., J. Hills and H. Sutherland (2009), 'Poverty, inequality and redistribution', in J. Hills, T. Sefton and K. Stewart (eds), *Towards a More Equal Society? Poverty, inequality and policy since 1997*, Bristol: Policy Press.

Shackleton, J. R. (2002), *Employment Tribunals: Their Growth and the Case for Radical Reform*, London: Institute of Economic Affairs.

Shackleton, J. R. (2005), 'The labour market under New Labour: the first two terms', *Economic Affairs*, 25(3): 31–8.

Shackleton, J. R. (2011), 'Education, training and childcare', in P. Booth (ed.), *Sharper Axes, Lower Taxes. Big steps to a smaller state*, London: Institute of Economic Affairs.

Simon, A. and E. Whiting (2007), 'Using the FRS to examine employment trends of couples', *Economic and Labour Market Review*, 1(11): 41–7.

Sinai, T. and J. Waldfogel (2005), 'Do low-income housing subsidies increase the occupied housing stock?', *Journal of Public Economics*, 89(11/12): 2137–64.

Sinclair, M. (2011), *Let Them Eat Carbon: The price of failing climate change policies, and how governments and Big Business profit from them*, Hull: Biteback Publishing.

Skedinger, P. (2010), *Employment Protection Legislation: Evolution, effects, winners and losers*, Cheltenham: Edward Elgar.

Smith, D. (2011), 'The changing economic role of government: past, present and prospective', in P. Booth (ed.), *Sharper Axes, Lower Taxes. Big steps to a smaller state*, London: Institute of Economic Affairs.

Snowdon, C. (2012a), *The Wages of Sin Taxes*, London: Adam Smith Institute.

Snowdon, C. (2012b), 'Sock puppets. How the government lobbies itself and why', IEA Discussion Paper no. 39, London: Institute of Economic Affairs.

Statistische Ämter des Bundes und der Länder (2011), *Statistikportal*, Data set: 'Gebiet und Bevölkerung, Fläche und Bevölkerung'.

Stern, N. (2007), *The Economics of Climate Change: The Stern Review*, Cambridge: Cambridge University Press.

Stewart, K., T. Sefton and J. Hills (2009), 'Introduction', in J. Hills, T. Sefton and K. Stewart (eds), *Towards a More Equal Society? Poverty, inequality and policy since 1997*, Bristol: Policy Press.

Strulik, H., J. Tyran and P. Vanini (2006), 'Staying on the dole', Discussion Papers 06–18, Department of Economics, University of Copenhagen.

Thies, C. and S. Porche (2007), 'The political economy of agricultural protection', *Journal of Politics*, 69(1): 116–27.

Townsend, J. (1996), 'Price and consumption of tobacco', *British Medical Bulletin*, 52(1): 132–42.

Truss, E. (2012), 'Affordable quality: new approaches to childcare', London: Centre Forum.

UK National Ecosystem Assessment (2011), *The UK National Ecosystem Assessment: Synthesis of the Key Findings*, Cambridge: UNEP-WCMC.

UNICEF (2005), 'Child poverty in rich countries', Report Card 6, Innocenti Research Centre, Florence: UNICEF.

UNICEF (2012), 'Measuring child poverty', New league tables of child poverty in the world's rich countries, Report Card 10, Innocenti Research Centre, Florence: UNICEF.

Urwin, P. (2011), *Self-Employment, Small Firms and Enterprise*, London: Institute of Economic Affairs.

uSwitch (2011), *uSwitch Quality of Life Index: UK the worst place to live in Europe*, available at http://www.uswitch.com/news/

money/uswitch-quality-of-life-index-uk-is-the-worst-place-to-live-in-europe-900002286/.

Veit-Wilson, J. (2007), 'Minimum income – myths and realities', EAPN Campaign for Adequate Minimum Income.

Von Mises, L. (1956: this edition 1994), *The Anti-Capitalistic Mentality*, Grove City: Libertarian Press.

Wallis, E. (ed.) (2012), *The Fairness Instinct. How we can harness public opinion to save the environment*, London: Fabian Society.

West London Free School (2011), 'The free schools revolution', WLFS blog, available at http://www.westlondonfreeschool.co.uk/blog/the-free-schools-revolution.html.

Whaples, R. (2009), 'The policy views of American Economic Association members: the results of a new survey', *Econ Journal Watch*, 6(3): 337–48, American Institute for Economic Research.

Wilkinson, R. and K. Pickett (2009), *The Spirit Level. Why More Equal Societies Almost Always Do Better*, London: Penguin.

Woodward, L. (1965), *The Age of Reform: 1815–1870*, Oxford History of England, 2nd edn, New York: Oxford University Press.

World Bank (2011a), 'Poverty headcount ratio at $2 a day (PPP) (% of population)', Data set, available at http://data.worldbank.org/indicator/SI.POV.2DAY.

World Bank (2011b), 'Data on trade and import barriers, trends in average MFN applied tariff rates in developing and industrial countries', Data set, available at http://go.worldbank.org/LGOXFTV550.

World Bank (2012a), PovcalNet, an online poverty analysis tool, available at http://iresearch.worldbank.org/PovcalNet/index.htm.

World Bank (2012b), 'Agriculture, value added (% of GDP)', Data set, available at http://data.worldbank.org/indicator/NV.AGR.TOTL.ZS.

World Bank (2012c), 'Agriculture value added per worker (constant 2000 US$)', Data set, available at http://data.worldbank.org/indicator/EA.PRD.AGRI.KD.

Wu, C., M. Cancian, D. Meyer and G. Wallace (2004), 'How do welfare sanctions work?', Discussion Paper no. 1282–04, Institute for Research on Poverty.

ABOUT THE IEA

The Institute is a research and educational charity (No. CC 235 351), limited by guarantee. Its mission is to improve understanding of the fundamental institutions of a free society by analysing and expounding the role of markets in solving economic and social problems.

The IEA achieves its mission by:

- a high-quality publishing programme
- conferences, seminars, lectures and other events
- outreach to school and college students
- brokering media introductions and appearances

The IEA, which was established in 1955 by the late Sir Antony Fisher, is an educational charity, not a political organisation. It is independent of any political party or group and does not carry on activities intended to affect support for any political party or candidate in any election or referendum, or at any other time. It is financed by sales of publications, conference fees and voluntary donations.

In addition to its main series of publications the IEA also publishes a termly journal, *Economic Affairs*.

The IEA is aided in its work by a distinguished international Academic Advisory Council and an eminent panel of Honorary Fellows. Together with other academics, they review prospective IEA publications, their comments being passed on anonymously to authors. All IEA papers are therefore subject to the same rigorous independent refereeing process as used by leading academic journals.

IEA publications enjoy widespread classroom use and course adoptions in schools and universities. They are also sold throughout the world and often translated/reprinted.

Since 1974 the IEA has helped to create a worldwide network of 100 similar institutions in over 70 countries. They are all independent but share the IEA's mission.

Views expressed in the IEA's publications are those of the authors, not those of the Institute (which has no corporate view), its Managing Trustees, Academic Advisory Council members or senior staff.

Members of the Institute's Academic Advisory Council, Honorary Fellows, Trustees and Staff are listed on the following page.

The Institute gratefully acknowledges financial support for its publications programme and other work from a generous benefaction by the late Alec and Beryl Warren.

251

Other papers recently published by the IEA include:

Taxation and Red Tape
The Cost to British Business of Complying with the UK Tax System
Francis Chittenden, Hilary Foster & Brian Sloan
Research Monograph 64; ISBN 978 0 255 36612 0; £12.50

Ludwig von Mises – A Primer
Eamonn Butler
Occasional Paper 143; ISBN 978 0 255 36629 8; £7.50

Does Britain Need a Financial Regulator?
Statutory Regulation, Private Regulation and Financial Markets
Terry Arthur & Philip Booth
Hobart Paper 169; ISBN 978 0 255 36593 2; £12.50

Hayek's *The Constitution of Liberty*
An Account of Its Argument
Eugene F. Miller
Occasional Paper 144; ISBN 978 0 255 36637 3; £12.50

Fair Trade Without the Froth
A Dispassionate Economic Analysis of 'Fair Trade'
Sushil Mohan
Hobart Paper 170; ISBN 978 0 255 36645 8; £10.00

A New Understanding of Poverty
Poverty Measurement and Policy Implications
Kristian Niemietz
Research Monograph 65; ISBN 978 0 255 36638 0; £12.50

The Challenge of Immigration
A Radical Solution
Gary S. Becker
Occasional Paper 145; ISBN 978 0 255 36613 7; £7.50

Sharper Axes, Lower Taxes
Big Steps to a Smaller State
Edited by Philip Booth
Hobart Paperback 38; ISBN 978 0 255 36648 9; £12.50

Self-employment, Small Firms and Enterprise
Peter Urwin
Research Monograph 66; ISBN 978 0 255 36610 6; £12.50

Crises of Governments
The Ongoing Global Financial Crisis and Recession
Robert Barro
Occasional Paper 146; ISBN 978 0 255 36657 1; £7.50

... and the Pursuit of Happiness
Wellbeing and the Role of Government
Edited by Philip Booth
Readings 64; ISBN 978 0 255 36656 4; £12.50

Public Choice – A Primer
Eamonn Butler
Occasional Paper 147; ISBN 978 0 255 36650 2; £10.00

The Profit Motive in Education: Continuing the Revolution
Edited by James B. Stanfield
Readings 65; ISBN 978 0 255 36646 5; £12.50

Which Road Ahead – Government or Market?
Oliver Knipping & Richard Wellings
Hobart Paper 171; ISBN 978 0 255 36619 9; £10.00

The Future of the Commons
Beyond Market Failure and Government Regulation
Elinor Ostrom et al.
Occasional Paper 148; ISBN 978 0 255 36653 3; £10.00

Other IEA publications

Comprehensive information on other publications and the wider work of the IEA can be found at www.iea.org.uk. To order any publication please see below.

Personal customers

Orders from personal customers should be directed to the IEA:
Clare Rusbridge
IEA
2 Lord North Street
FREEPOST LON10168
London SW1P 3YZ
Tel: 020 7799 8907. Fax: 020 7799 2137
Email: crusbridge@iea.org.uk

Trade customers

All orders from the book trade should be directed to the IEA's distributor:
Gazelle Book Services Ltd (IEA Orders)
FREEPOST RLYS-EAHU-YSCZ
White Cross Mills
Hightown
Lancaster LA1 4XS
Tel: 01524 68765. Fax: 01524 53232
Email: sales@gazellebooks.co.uk

IEA subscriptions

The IEA also offers a subscription service to its publications. For a single annual payment (currently £42.00 in the UK), subscribers receive every monograph the IEA publishes. For more information please contact:
Clare Rusbridge
Subscriptions
IEA
2 Lord North Street
FREEPOST LON10168
London SW1P 3YZ
Tel: 020 7799 8907. Fax: 020 7799 2137
Email: crusbridge@iea.org.uk